REFLECTIONS ON A TOUR DU MONT BLANC

**

TIME OUT WITH A BEAR

K.R. ALLCOAT
& Chorkie Walker

Busco Books

ISBN 978-1699999639
Published by Busco Books
Lloret de Mar, Spain
2020

For my Mum,
and for the child in all of us

Day 0: Once upon a Time

The coach pulled out of the station forty minutes late and I tried to quell the niggling fear that I would miss my connection in Geneva, twelve hours from now, telling myself I was on the scheduled coach, and there was nothing I could do to prevent further delays. If we were going to be late, it was up to the bus company to get me to Chamonix-Mont Blanc.

It was still daylight outside and midnight was almost three hours away. I wouldn't sleep for all that was buzzing round my head, so I looked up Chamonix on my phone, but found it hard to concentrate on other people's facts and figures. Switching back to airplane mode, to save battery power, I sat back to think freely about what I had let myself in for: nine and two half-days of trekking and camping alone, in an attempt to complete the Tour du Mont Blanc (TMB), one of the world's *Grandes Randonnées* (great walks), a challenging 170km of hiking with almost 10,000m of elevation (106 miles, 32,800 ft).

I'm not your typical hiker, though it's not for me to say: a middle-aged-and-confused male who smokes (6–8 per day), and enjoys foods high in fat and starch and drinks high in sugar. I have an arthritic condition known as ankylosing spondylitis (AS) which can cause chronic pain, as well as acute. I favour occasional activity over regular exercise, with the odd game of playground cricket during the winter, the occasional park'n'cycle ride, and probably no more than 10km on foot per week, much to the frustration of my rheumatologist. I lead quite an active life as a carpenter when I can get the work, but a lazy life whenever my condition allows me to be comfortable. I am not ambitious nor ever have been, mostly content to muddle along leading a low-impact life, with occasional outbreaks of feverish activity.

Despite my father's attempts to bring out the boisterous in me, I was never a keen boy scout. I was too introspective to be aware of nature and practical things. I liked playing sports, but I wasn't much good at

them, so I never got picked for any school teams. He took the family camping every summer, mostly to seaside sites. The journey there was always long and tiresome, for we lived in central England, as far from the seaside as it's possible to be. I preferred digging holes in the sand to sunbathing and swimming, so I was bored until we eventually went to the Lake District. We climbed the *Old Man of Coniston* as a family, but we never hiked anywhere with a tent. Perhaps we might have, if my father had not been killed when I was 11.

My mother re-married, and I took up cycle touring with my step-brother. A three-week tour of some of Scotland and Northern England's highest and steepest mountain roads, overnighting in youth hostels, preceded our month-long 2,500km ride to Lake Geneva and back, visiting six European countries outside the UK, all on a meagre budget.

I started University as a willing but naïve student of Economics with an innate understanding of mathematics and logic. The impulse purchase of Edward de Bono's *Lateral Thinking*, in a Lancaster bookshop, however, made me begin to question the assumptions of the market economy as a means to bring order to the chaos of nature. It generally involved ransacking the earth and its creatures for short-term gain, with scant regard for the obscene amounts of long-term waste generated in the process. There had to be a better way.

I enjoyed a good social life at University, with five or six exclusive groups of friends that I would meet with separately: flatmates, future flatmates, fellow skiers, and students from each faculty. But the wearing of so many faces wore me down and, with my changing frame of mind, I abandoned them all for one, rather depressed.

I graduated, but never reconciled with the prospect of getting a proper job, and thought I could serve the world as a writer. My mother said that I needed to gain some more life experience before I could hope to write well and be read.

Determined to do it my way, I left home with my tired pushbike in search of inspiration and a gap year. Riding 1,000km in eight days, I couldn't keep up with the repairs I had to make and we burned out together in Grenoble, France. After another two weeks of soul-searching, there and in Paris, I took the bike back home on the train and resolved never to rely on one for holiday transport ever again.

One week later, I visited the same Lancaster bookshop and was struck by the cover of a book: *Wandering*, by Hermann Hesse (Picador, ISBN 0330244205). It shows a prisoner stepping through the painting he has made on his cell wall, and out onto an Alpine footpath. It resonated with my fear of the nine-to-five prison, so I bought it, on impulse, with the high hope that it might teach me the secret of escape. I sat and read it whilst staying overnight with a friend whose flat was across the road from the shop. Its prose and poetry tell of the middle-aged author's musings, as with mixed feelings he says farewell to his German homeland and crosses an Alpine pass into Switzerland. After exorcising his contempt for borders and wars, he tells of his love for nature and the rustic life, and of his wistful struggle with life's contradictions. It carried me away until the moment I looked up from the book, and found myself back in the prison again.

A few days later, I moved in with said friend, only to discover that he was paying no rent and that we were effectively squatting. For several months I lived the life of a decadent surrealist poet, reading and revelling, and seized every opportunity to go wild camping.

After being evicted, I returned home to work as a delivery driver, then moved to London where I met my wife-to-be. I took her camping, continued to read, and temped my way into the publishing industry. I quit my job there and we moved to the West Country where I walked into a position selling newspaper advertising. We married, bought a house and then I lost my job for lack of faith in the product. I took up typesetting and secured a union-approved job, and after two years, started night-schooling to learn carpentry. Our daughter was born, I quit my job and took up carpentry, sold up and moved to North Devon. When recession hit in the early 1990's, I had to do a bit of this and a bit of that, which came to include evening and weekend work at a second hand bookshop. After years of wandering through life, I began to think I had found my niche, and volunteered for all the hours I could get.

Within three years I opened my own shop, funded on a shoestring. It went so well that, as I developed it online, I saw an opportunity to sell up and move to the Costa Brava, Spain, with wife, two children and 5,000 books. It wasn't long before I opened another shop there.

After nine years, the cumulative effect on my profitability of the banking crisis, smartphones, and A.online reaching critical mass, put an end to my aspirations as a bricks-and-mortar retailer. I submitted defeat and returned to wood-work.

Several difficult years of sporadic work followed, in which I tried to write a novel. I thought I'd cracked it in 2017, with *Wood For The Trees*, but it was unreadable. Everything else I wrote took on an ever-evolving plot, with no particular direction, and no limits to where it might go, with no end in sight. I needed an idea to limit my aspirations.

In May 2018, I started on a new contract, making wooden cabins. At the beginning of August, I was offered my first wage-paid summer holiday for thirty years.

I wanted to get as far away as possible from the screaming wail of machinery cutting timber. Or was it the timber screaming? My wife was working part-time, her camping days were over, and she wasn't keen on what I had in mind – hiking in the Alps – so I was on my own.

Overnight coaches ran from my home town and could take me to Chamonix-Mont Blanc with only one change, much cheaper than flying. I searched online for some guidance of where I might go once I got there and was led straight to the Tour du Mont Blanc, a way-marked trail circumnavigating the birthplace of alpine sports, with up to three border crossings over Alpine passes. It was the perfect opportunity for me to combine several threads of interest without treading too far out of my comfort zone. Except, wild camping was not normally permitted in the region, and camp sites were few and far between. Some more research was needed.

There are more than one hundred *Grandes Randonnées* in Europe and the GR TMB is one of the greatest. It attracts tens of thousands of visitors each year. The official website, autourdumontblanc.com, is an ideal port of call for updates on weather conditions, as well as being a useful portal for booking refuges. Aside from that, there are a multitude of commercial agents offering tours etc, and bloggers telling of their personal experiences walking the TMB. Some of these offer advice to those that are thinking of doing it for themselves, some self-guided, some as part of a guided tour, but almost all make overnight stays in refuges, *auberges* or hotels. Few seem geared to campers.

There are no shortage of recommendations as to what kit the inexperienced hiker should carry, often with links to where you can buy them. If I had followed their advice, I could have spent several thousands on lightweight clothing and unnecessary equipment – I felt many a close call with affiliate marketing.

It was looking more like a rich person's indulgence than a humble person's escape. My self-imposed budget was 500€ all-inclusive, so I realised that I would have to rely on my own experience as a camper and not rely too much on others for guidance.

With only three weeks to organise myself, I needed to buy a tent and a good rucksack, as well as a decent raincoat. With a guide book and map, my total spend on new equipment before leaving amounted to 320€, some of which was covered by birthday gift donations – for the man who has nothing and still doesn't know what he wants. The rest of my equipment (including walking boots and sleeping bag) was old but usable, and my clothing came straight out of my wardrobe.

The transfer to Chamonix by coach cost me 151€, and I allowed myself 200€ cash to cover camp sites and food.

My first day was wasted through indecision, but I went on to walk anti-clockwise from Les Houches, France (near Chamonix), across several passes before arriving in Italy, a border crossing which was worthy of Hessean poetry.

The next day I encountered the annual Ultra-Tour du Mont Blanc (UTMB), a series of super-marathons run by up to 10,000 contestants in each race.

Two days later, I arrived at the Swiss border and crossed into limbo. Visibility was down to about 10m due to low cloud, and some approaching hikers reported they'd seen nothing for miles, so with a sense of anti-climax I turned round and headed back to my camp site, awestruck by a fresh wave of competitors running uphill towards me.

Next day I took the local bus back through the tunnel to Chamonix to rest and get a good meal, only to find the town packed with people and in festival mood. The headline 170km race was concluding with course times of around 22 hours. Bar and restaurant staff were overwhelmed with customers, making it easier for me to go bar squatting on the peripheries, until I eventually got noticed each time and was invited to buy something.

Allowing for the gift donations and some cash overspend on the trail, my week's break cost around 600€, or just 379€ not including reusable equipment. It had been an unforgettable adventure and I was determined to return soon with another 500€.

After eleven months of anticipation, the time had come, and, from the moment I stepped off the connecting coach in Chamonix-Mont Blanc in the morning to the moment I caught the return ten days and eight hours later, I would be escaping from the prison cell of responsibility to no one but myself, not forgetting my backpacking companion, Chorkie.

**

Twilight was upon us as we turned off the motorway towards the city of Girona. By the time we reached the bus station, the city centre sky was dark. The coach went underground, into a crisp concrete maze, deserted at this late hour except for a mother with children waiting to board and a man giving the children a farewell hug. Two backpackers appeared from behind a grey pillar, loaded their packs in the luggage hold and boarded. Once everyone was accounted for and seated, the flickering lights and the waving man were the only sign of life out there – a more depressing place I could not imagine someone to be left alone in. It was a relief when we re-surfaced to where the sky is unbound, even if obscured by light pollution.

I acted in haste when I reserved this coach, snatching what I thought was a good price whilst it lasted, only to realise once my card was charged that it was listed in pounds not euros. Aside from the currency discrepancy, it was only later that I noticed that starting from Chamonix added further complications.

I didn't want to repeat the first few days that I walked before, in case I couldn't complete the circuit. So, after discarding the idea of going through the tunnel and starting from Courmayeur, I decided to go clockwise, as what you lose on the ups you gain on the downs.

Going clockwise from Les Houches on the first day, however, would involve a monster climb of more than 1500m to the peak of Le Brévent, followed by a couple more hours to the first permitted bivouac site, at Refuge La Flégère. With my coach arriving in Chamonix at 9.30 a.m., I would not likely arrive at Les Houches until mid-morning. So, when I

THE TOUR DU MONT BLANC
Showing principal places of interest for guidance only

learned that the refuge was closed for the season and that camping was not going to be permitted, I had to re-think my plans.

My two half-days could be used to good effect if I took the cable car from Chamonix to Plan Praz, at 2000m above mean sea level (amsl), a ski station on the TMB route halfway between Le Brévent (2526m amsl) and La Flégère. From Plan Praz, it is only around 9km to Refuge Lac Blanc, where I could camp wild, according to their website.

The only drawback was that I wanted to use some of the many variants to the main TMB route over the following two days, so I wouldn't reach a grocery store without a significant detour for almost three days. I would need to carry three days' supply of food from the start.

For my final half-day, I would need to climb Le Brévent from Les Houches and descend a little to Plan Praz in order to be back in Chamonix by 5 p.m. for my coach home. If I could get to Les Houches on schedule, then I would know how early to set off for Le Brévent.

I could broadly follow the guide book's suggestions (see below) for the intermediate stages but, because I had already walked half the TMB, I would try to use a variant path where I had used the standard path before, and vice versa, with one notable exception.

The official path, clockwise, descends south-westwards from the Col de la Seigne (2,516m amsl) on the IT–FR border, and lands 1,000m below at Les Chapieux. Bivouac camping is permitted there. The next day involves climbing the 1,000m back up, northwards, to the Col de la Croix du Bonhomme (2,483m amsl) before going a similar amount back down to Les Contamines-Montjoie, where there is an official camp site and town. I wanted to avoid all that down and up.

Last year I had cut Les Chapieux out by using the variant from near the Col de la Croix du Bonhomme and slept wild at altitude. This year, I found a higher short-cut to bypass Les Chapieux, but it is not recommended for inexperienced hikers, and therefore not an official

variant. It tracks north-west from the Col de la Seigne along the ridge, maintaining height before dropping suddenly to the Lacs Jovet, a popular place to visit that I missed last time round. The Refuge Robert Blanc (2,750m amsl) is halfway along that path, so was ideally placed for my purposes. Camping is impractical because it is surrounded by rocks, but a bed-only reservation would cost me only 17€, so I booked this one and only night's stay to lock in my schedule. The half-board option cost only a further 28€, so I provisionally reserved a seat at the table, as a late birthday treat.

I took out my phone to remind myself of my chosen route. I would be re-covering only 37km of last year's 85km.

	Km*	hrs*	m*
Day 0: 20.30 Bus–Geneva–Chamonix, arrive 9.30			
Day 1: Plan Praz–Lac Blanc, FR (bivouac)	9	3	480
Day 2: Lac Blanc–Ref. Les Grands, CH (bivouac)	18	7	1150
Day 3: Ref. Les Grands–Champex d'Arpette, CH (camp site)	13	6.5	1082
Day 4: Champex d'Arpette–Le Fouly, CH (camp site)	15	4	500
Day 5: Le Fouly–Arp Nuova, IT (bus to camp site)	16	5.5	1150
Day 6: Arp Nuova–Courmayeur, IT (same camp site)	20	6.5	1000
Day 7: Courmayeur–Lago Combal, IT (same camp site)	17	5.5	875
Day 8: Lago Combal–Ref. Robert Blanc, FR (refuge)	15	7	900
Day 9: Ref. Robert Blanc–Les Contamines, FR (camp site)	14	6	350
Day 10: Les Contamines–Les Houches, FR (camp site)	19	5.5	633
Day 11: Les Houches–Plan Praz, FR (coach home)	17	5.5	1546
Day 12: Home			
Totals	173	62	9666

* All distances (km), times (hrs), and elevations (m), are taken either from *Trekking the Tour of Mont Blanc* by Kev Reynolds (Cicerone, 2015 edition, ISBN 978-1852847791) and/or estimated from the IGN TMB 1:50,000 map (ISBN 978-2758540946). Timings are based on non-stop walking and don't allow for rest breaks and photo-stops.

**

The coach left the motorway again and we drew into Figueres bus station, above ground, but once again without character in the darkness. We picked up a few passengers, bringing the coach to around half-full, and returned to the motorway, north towards the French border.

**

My only concession to going lightweight last year was to buy a compact set of pans for cooking. I over-packed on spare clothes and, consequently, my rucksack weighed too much to be comfortable. On my return, I weighed everything. It must have been 20kg including water. I was determined not to make the same mistake again and began listing and weighing every item that I would need this summer back in March, trying to scale it back.

One blogger suggested that anything over 12kg was too much, but, of course, they weren't camping. Another suggested that anything over 20% of one's body weight was unhealthy. (I weigh around 73kg, so that would limit me to 14.6kg). For every weight saving on equipment, clothes and toiletries, there were other things too important to leave out. Concerned with safety, I bought an emergency blanket and a whistle. Sitting on hard ground in the evenings after a hard day's walk is no fun when you've a bony bum and aching muscles, so I ordered a lightweight folding camping chair online, but it wasn't fit for purpose and I secured a refund. I settled for some rescued foam from a chair repair which would be expendable.

A ten-day supply of staple foods and toiletries added 50% extra to what would have been needed for seven, but I made savings by measuring more carefully and by using lighter weight and/or disposable containers.

Pasta, noodles and rice are often quoted as the staple food of many hikers, but I preferred to rely on bread for the carbohydrates. It works in a ham sandwich, in a jam sandwich, as a sponge for re-hydrated soup, it goes well with meats, eggs or cheese, and requires no boiling water to prepare. Bread is one of the easiest food items to replace, but I still needed plenty to begin with.

Ultimately, I shed nearly 3kg of dead weight and added an extra 1kg of food, so by the time I disembarked from the coach in Chamonix, my pack would weigh over 18kg, including water. By the fourth day, I anticipated it to hover around 15kg for the rest of the Tour. Having eaten everything and by discarding tired equipment and toiletries on the final morning, I hoped to carry a pack below 12kg to the end. [See *Appendix* for the full packing list.]

**

The coach pulled off again, this time at a service *area*. The co-driver announced that we would have to be back on board in twenty minutes. It was a good opportunity for a final stretch of the legs, so I used the loo, finished my flask of tea and bacon sandwiches, and had a smoke.

The stop took longer than twenty minutes, as the drivers enjoyed a full meal whilst the passengers waited patiently. We lost yet more time when we stopped for a refill of diesel – so that was probably my connection missed for sure, but, what can you do?

The next stop would be Perpignan, 30km across the

border, no more than half an hour away, so it wasn't worth trying to settle before then.

**

The coach transfer shouldn't have cost me more than 161€, but my booking error pushed it to 175€. Allowing for the extra nights' camping, I had expanded my cash budget to 300€ (or 250€ + 50CF). So I was still budgeting to complete the tour with less than 500€, not including reusable equipment and clothing.

Other new equipment included good walking socks and quality plasters, a lightweight sleeping bag, and a pair of lightweight trousers, amounting to less than 100€. Upgrades to everyday items, like a thermos flask, and a smartphone with a good resolution camera, inbuilt altimeter and compass, I would have replaced anyway.

Back in 2001, when I told friends that I was moving to Spain with my family, one said *how lucky*, as if we had won the lottery. But luck had no more to do with that than it did with anything else. Life throws opportunities one's way all the time and I haven't always taken those that came to me, some because I was slow on the uptake, and some because I chose not to pursue them. But once I decide something is worth doing, I set my mind to it and go for it, just as I set my mind on doing this TMB, without any training, with very little experience, very little money, and no special kit. I'm not afraid of swimming against the tide of modern opinions about needing all the latest gear, and I wasn't about to abandon all hygiene and comfort for the sake of a few grams. I've spent too much of my life questioning conformity, but giving in to popular opinion for a quiet life.

When I recently met with a friend I told him about my plans and he didn't understand, as there are some beautiful hikes in the Pyrenees, so, why go all the way to the Alps?

Mont Blanc is the highest mountain in Western Europe, I answered, and I've been drawn to it since I was a child. Everest is the highest mountain in the world, and I would love to go to the Himalayas, but think I should start in the Alps and see how that goes. Perhaps I'll look at the Pyrenees in between times.

Concerned for my mediocre health and my smoking habit, he wondered if I should have such lofty ideals to do the whole 170km of the TMB.

I've done half of it, so, why not the whole of it? I felt I knew my strengths and recognised my limitations, and I'm not getting any younger. If not now, then, when? Camping and trekking should not just be for fitness fanatics, bucket-listers and the wealthy middle-ages concerned about their health.

Who knows, perhaps I could write a blog of my own?

**

Despite the late hour, Perpignan bus station seemed much brighter and more cheerful than anywhere since being on the coach, but it was a relief to get back on the main road. I could finally get a couple of hours undisturbed sleep, so long as we went directly to Avignon without further stops. Roaming charges in Switzerland are expensive, and, even though I would not sleep that far, I double-checked that my phone was in airplane mode, closed my eyes, yawned, and began to drift.

**

Chorkie is a cream-coloured teddy bear with a rucksack, standing 12cm tall. He was originally a souvenir from York Castle Museum, c.2006, product coded *YORKWALK*. When gifted, he was indifferently referred to as Yorkie and used to brighten up a shop shelf. When the shop closed, he was put back on another shelf and actively ignored until quite recently.

As luck would have it, the wonders of technology had granted Conkers, a retired and disabled air-freshener bear with his own quad bike, the opportunity of an Instagram account. In the spring of 2019, he invited Yorkie to accompany him on his adventures on the road, to visit the places he could not for, unlike Conkers, Yorkie still had the use of his legs and could go off the beaten track.

The invitation was all Yorkie needed to free himself from the shackles of slavery and boredom. Legend had it that his ancestry was Swiss, so he discarded his ribbon of shame, went bare, and changed his name to Chorkie Walker.

If his cherished chum Conkers is chestnut and cheesy, then charming and cheerful, Chorkie is cheeky.

Together they are #conkersnchorkie, with their own occasional blog at bearsontheroad.travel.blog.

Day 1: Arrival

Every now and then, a subtle shift in G-forces woke me during the night, as the coach slowed for toll booths, or entered a bus station. I remembered Avignon and Montpelier, but I must have slept through Grenoble and any others. Whilst it was dark it was easy to get back to sleep each time.

When I awoke during daylight, we were leaving the motorway. I took out my phone to check the time: 7.40a.m. Perhaps we were going to cross the border into Switzerland. There was still time to make my 08.30 connection.

But we didn't. Instead, we entered a French border town by the name of Annemasse, which I later learned is peopled with commuters that can't afford to live in Geneva. We turned into anonymous streets, with empty wasteland and graffitied hoardings providing the only contrast to the concrete monotone of the buildings and shuttered shops. Eventually we stopped in a non-descript area to set down a couple of passengers. We moved off again and I was left wondering why all these bus stops and stations were so depressing.

Leaving the built-up centre, we went a couple more kilometres on a main road before arriving at the Swiss frontier. The co-driver left the coach, presumably to attend to customs bureaucracy. Ten minutes later and we were still there, waiting. This might take a while.

I reopened the cached pages I'd looked at last night on the place in Chamonix where I had arranged to meet Chorkie. He and Conkers had visited Courmayeur in Italy the previous week, on a whistle-stop tour which included the Alps. Before Conkers drove home to Catalunya he dropped off Chorkie, who then made his own way to rendezvous with me, his porter for our Tour du Mont Blanc.

I must have dozed off, for the driver was back and he'd been gone forty minutes. The screen was black, but the pages were still open on my phone.

In a nutshell, I learned that the bronze statue in the centre of the Place Balmat, Chamonix-Mont Blanc, is dedicated to the centenary of the ascent of Mont Blanc made in 1787 by financier Horace Bénédict de Saussure, chamois hunter and crystal collector Jacques Balmat, and a party of eighteen servants carrying supplies and scientific equipment. It depicts Saussure and Balmat, with the latter pointing excitedly towards the summit of the mountain.

Jacques Balmat had already claimed the prize offered by Saussure for the race proper to the summit in 1786. On that historic occasion, he accompanied Michel-Gabriel Paccard, a Chamonix doctor, who had already made several failed attempts to carry a barometer to the summit, accompanied by others. He was only in it for the science, and, with Balmat's help, carried all his own equipment. Paccard had to wait for the bicentenary of his achievement to get a statue of his own, 150m away and out of sight. Fascinating.

The contrast between the buildings and shops of Geneva and those of Annemasse was extreme: from Art Nouveau town houses to post-war concrete tower blocks, from premium boutiques to discount warehouses, from quality watch stores to mobile phone shops.

We eventually pulled into Geneva bus station around 9.15 a.m., two hours behind schedule, an hour late for my connection to Chamonix. I retrieved my rucksack from the hold and went into the ticket office to ask for help.

The officer there spoke perfect English and knew who I was – she had been calling for me over the tannoy an hour beforehand. The delay was the fault of the coach service, so she suggested I buy a new ticket to Chamonix and make a claim from E.lines, at the email address she gave me.

E.lines? I bought my ticket through an English agent, O.travel, and the Spanish coach provider was A.bus. I was expecting a French O.bus to take me to Chamonix. No wonder I overpaid, with so many intermediaries involved. That'll teach me.

She offered me a seat on an F.bus coach, due in about twenty minutes. It would cost me 18€, much less than the 30€ I had originally been charged for this part of the journey several months ago. The prospect of an extra refund and a quick departure eased my frustration, so I paid in cash. It seemed the service continued on through the tunnel to Courmayeur and Turin at not much of an extra cost, so I made a mental note to consider them for any future coach journeys.

Alas, it too arrived behind schedule, having come from Zurich, albeit by only twenty minutes.

At the border, customs officials boarded and checked everyone's passports for themselves. It seemed strange to me that coaches from Spain and other parts of the EU should find it beneficial to make connections here, where the Schengen zone does not extend. Border checks must cause innumerable delays, and multiple claims for refunds for missed connections.

Once we were safely back in France again, I fingered a quick email to E.lines to register my complaint and checked my messages.

We passed through stunning scenery, and entered Chamonix just before 11.30 a.m. I pulled out my rucksack and walked away without delay. The Place Balmat was as good as any place to commemorate the start of this adventure, as it's just a brisk five-minute walk from the bus

station. But, like Balmat before him, Chorkie had gotten in with a selfie first and stolen the glory from this diarist.

I was tired from insufficient sleep and two hours late, so I scooped up my passenger, and we headed north across town towards the cable car station. I walked past the church and tried to pick out the Plan Praz station, as it should be right there in front of me, but it was hidden beneath cloud.

The views elsewhere and all around, even from down here (1035m amsl), were appetite-whetting, and the ten minute walk to the edge of the town up a gentle gradient provided a pleasant warm-up for what was to come.

The price one way was 14.50€, open return 18.50€. The potential saving was tempting, but I couldn't be sure of meeting my self-imposed schedule in order to take advantage of it. Perhaps it would enthuse me with extra incentive? For 4€ extra I could have a free ride at the end of my Tour. Chances were, I would be broke in ten days' time, so I paid the 18.50€, cash, in keeping with the axiom to *leave no trace*. At least I would only have myself to blame if I missed this connection.

Cars run continuously, so once you have your ticket you get straight on and go. They fit up to six people with bags or skis, and I followed two people into one when I might have waited for an empty car – with their paraglider backpacks already on the floor there was barely room for me to put my pack down, but they shuffled up and we made do.

The ride took five minutes, so by 12.15 p.m. I was stepping out at 2000m amsl, and walking uphill to where the Tour du Mont Blanc threads past the head of Plan Praz.

Once I had found the familiar signposts showing the path I needed – to La Flégère 1h 15mins – I looked for a suitable place to stand my gas stove and pan. A dormant ski lift station nearby provided shelter from the wind, and I set up on a conveniently-placed concrete ledge. I took out a half-litre bottle of water to make the tea with and was pleased to see it was still half-frozen. All but the lump went in my small saucepan for the boil. The other bottle in my bag was also still half-frozen so, together, they ought to keep refrigerating to the evening.

I had a late breakfast of muesli and milk, and prepared a tuna sandwich to follow.

Despite being in the thick of ski stations and pylons, the scenery beyond them was staggeringly beautiful. Paragliders fell and rose again before disappearing somewhere into the valley below – it looked like fun, though I'm not sure I would have the nerve. The Aiguille du Midi cable car station sat precariously on a peak at 3842m amsl, stark against the clear blue sky. It forms part of the second quickest overland route between Chamonix, France, and Courmayeur, Italy. It can cost a tidy three-figure sum per person, and that's only one-way. The local bus through the tunnel is quicker, and considerably cheaper at 15€ one-way.

After an earlier sighting of the peak, clouds came back to disguise Mont Blanc.

Cake and a couple of biscuits followed the sandwich, all washed down with the tea. My legs were ready to go, having spent most of the past eighteen hours scrunched up. Chorkie was belted into a side pocket of my pack and I was on the trail just after 1 p.m.

Once away from the ski station, the 5km TMB path to Refuge La Flégère is green and lush on either side. It weaves in great curves to the left and right along the contours, with gentle ups and steeper downs, towards 1850m amsl.

A number of junctions gave me doubts, and, after taking the map out for the third time, I realised it would be much easier to keep my compass to hand and, wherever in doubt, follow a bearing North-East.

The relatively gentle gradients, combined with jaw-dropping views, made for an excellent introduction to the Tour. I reached La Flégère just after 4 p.m., but the refuge and ski station were cordoned off. Just

past it, I made my own diversion and turned left onto a steeply rising path towards Lac Blanc.

Lac Blanc was one of about ten highlighted targets on the TMB that I hadn't already visited. It lies on a variant route, and to reach it in the confines of the recommended day's stage is a tall order for most.

Its remoteness was only part of its attraction, however, for it is also reputed to be in a beautiful spot, with equally beautiful views. I wanted to spend the night there to catch the sunset, the sunrise, or both.

According to my map reading, the distance from La Flégère to Lac Blanc is 3km. Kev Reynolds says it should take 1h 30mins, and by my calculations there are 480m of elevation.

The continuous twists and turns are not clearly shown on the map, so, with an average gradient of 16%, it's no wonder it felt like I was climbing through mud. After an hour I tested the altimeter on my phone. It read barely 2020m amsl, meaning I was only just a third of the way. I was not physically prepared for this.

In day-to-day life I bound up

staircases two at a time. But with 25% of my body weight on my shoulders, my heart hammered in my chest and I had to stop regularly to catch my breath, or to check the map, to take a photo, to soak up the scenery, to give way to oncoming traffic, to take a drink, for any excuse.

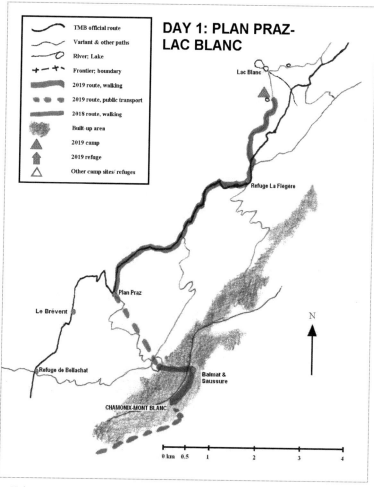

DAY 1: PLAN PRAZ-LAC BLANC

Legend:
- TMB official route
- Variant & other paths
- River; Lake
- Frontier; boundary
- 2019 route, walking
- 2019 route, public transport
- 2018 route, walking
- Built-up area
- 2019 camp
- 2019 refuge
- Other camp sites/ refuges

Lac Blanc

Refuge La Flégère

Plan Praz

Le Brévent

Refuge de Bellachat

Balmat & Saussure

CHAMONIX-MONT BLANC

N

0 km 0.5 1 2 3 4

Why was I punishing myself this way?, I wondered.

When asked why he wanted to climb Mount Everest, George Leigh-Mallory is reported to have said: *Because it's there.* He was a well-educated man, and the son of a clergyman, so his remark could be interpreted as a pithy reminder of mankind's never-ending thirst to go higher, bigger and better in all things, for personal or collective aggrandizement; or simply as arrogant words from an agent of destiny for mankind to overcome and subdue nature.

I chose to go hiking as a means to escape, to get a hands-on appreciation of the natural world for its own sake. Forcing the natural rhythms of the body to adhere to the clock, training for mechanical activity and adjusting to society are not healthy. As a smoker, I recognised the value of the fresh air too. Out here there is little or no industrial pollution. The air, like the water, is as pure as it can ever be. Putting my lungs to work in this atmosphere would help repair any self-inflicted damage. It was only after coming here last year that I caught the bug and saw an opportunity to challenge myself to achieve something for its own sake, for the self-aggrandizement.

Chorkie is quite photogenic so he's here to inject a little fun into my day, to stop me going mad.

Almost six hours after leaving Plan Praz, I happened upon a pair of wild campers beside a small pond and asked them how much further it was to the lake. With French accents they told me a half-hour's walk.

Like most of the people I had met that day, they were walking anti-clockwise, and had just come from Lac Blanc. If I understood them correctly, they told me camping by the lake or refuge is forbidden, but the warden of the refuge gave unofficial permission to camp in the environs. This was the first suitable place they'd come to, and there was nowhere any nearer on the path beyond the refuge.

I looked at the altimeter on my mobile phone, which read 2190m, around 160m short of the refuge.

With the time nearing 7.00 p.m., my legs complaining and my heart giving no respite, the opportunity to rest for the night was welcome. The view was still pretty spectacular, and the surrounding hills gave the site a sheltered feel, so I found a level patch of ground 8–10m from the Frenchmen, stripped off my boots and socks and set my feet free in the long, damp grass to discharge the last remnants of the electrical world. No sign of blisters, but it was early yet.

The Frenchmen went to bathe in the knee-deep pond and splashed about like children. I hadn't asked their names for I would only forget them. I have always had difficulty retaining spoken information and, I think, a kind of aural dyslexia – much better to see it written down. I could blame the only teacher I ever had at school whose lessons I enjoyed. He was the school psychologist and did a lot of sick relief for other teachers. Rather than following their lesson plan, he would just tell stories, usually with a lesson to be learned from them. *Believe nothing you hear and only half of what you see* became a motto he shared that I still live by.

Pitching my tent took longer than it should have for I had forgotten how it went up. This was a replacement tent from the one I used on last year's visit to Mont Blanc. It is a little heavier, but of a much better design and 40% cheaper. I'd used it only once before, in May, to satisfy my need for accommodation when I flew to England to attend the funeral of an old friend. He was a keen camper, and it was my way of paying my respects and getting some training. I hiked 55km fully laden across the gentle hills of Avon & Wiltshire in three days, on top of 13km unladen on the day of the funeral.

I looked up from my struggles and saw an ibex nearby, watching me and the others, nervously. I returned its gaze, looked about, and saw another a little further away. I took a few photos without getting too close to frighten them, and went back to my task. Finding the instructions tucked inside the tent bag helped considerably.

By the time it was up, my neighbours were preparing something to eat. They were clearly good friends and not interested in making any new ones for the evening. That didn't bother me, it suited me fine.

I went to the pond to wash my feet. The water wasn't dirty, but there didn't seem to be any sign of movement. It looked like a half empty puddle of rainwater that might dry up in a few days. I was put off taking water from it to drink, even if I were to boil it. [I later discovered that the pond is marked on the IGN map, too small to be named, but at least a recognised landmark. I'm still not sure if it is technically a lake.]

With Refuge La Flégère being closed, and nowhere else being available to pick up fresh water, all I had was the remains of the previously-frozen bottles. They had served well to keep cool the meat, the cheese and the milk and remained cool. I fried up some mince, onions and a tomato to eat with bread, and made two cups of tea: one for now and one for the flask to have later on. I had drunk all my cola during the afternoon walk. By the time I had finished, there was very

little fresh water left. I would have to wait till I reached the refuge in the morning for tea and breakfast beside the lake. I scoffed off some cake for dessert and stared across the pond.

There would be no life without water. And water needs to keep

circulating in order to sustain life. It can only keep circulating by rising as a gas and falling as a liquid or solid. If the world were flat, water would be stagnant with nowhere to run. Mountains provide the high points of land upon which water can fall from the clouds in its purest form as rain, gather into rivers, feed everything in its wake, and return to the ocean carrying all forms of debris to be broken down by the salty sea, only to be distilled once again by the action of evaporation.

The mountains are primordial, defiant, yet pliant to water and ice. The bigger or more weather-worn the mountain, the deeper it reaches into me on all levels, emotional, intellectual and spiritual. The sense and power of falling water is hypnotic and purifying.

That should be good enough reason for wanting to be here, for why I am willing to lug a heavy pack up and down the mountain trail rather than use my holiday time to lie in the sun by a chemical-filled pool sipping cocktails. I'm not here to identify plants or sample the local cuisine – I want to appreciate what I can for what it is, with the eyes of a child, not because it it features on a list of recommendations.

The neighbours had finished eating and were taking a walk towards an outcrop to watch the sun go down. I washed my pans and cutlery in the pond and left them tidy, picked up Chorkie and my flask, and followed their lead to find our own rocky outcrop.

We gazed at the view for an hour or so before the night began to draw down the light. Mont Blanc exposed itself momentarily to the naked evening sun *because it was there*, whilst the valleys below were already in twilight. More ibex approached us, from all sides, and backed away. The pond must surely be their territorial watering hole.

It was almost 10 p.m. by the time we returned to the tent.

I cleaned my teeth, had a pee, and got into my sleeping bag. I sent messages to my family, and Chorkie uploaded his day to Instagram and slept in the tent's inner pouch.

I was too tired to write up any kind of report of my day, so I turned off the phone to save the battery.

The Frenchmen had also retired, but were still chatting and giggling as I lay there trying to doze off. Eventually they and everything else fell quiet. No doubt the ibex would feel safe enough to approach for that drink in the stillness.

A more perfect spot to camp would have been hard to imagine.

Day 2: Photographer's Joy

Chorkie and I were walking up a mountain path together. I was trying to get a reading on my barometer, whilst he was stopping to pick up crystals, muttering something every time one went in his rucksack. I looked back at my barometer and the reading had gone from 1024 to 924. The quartz is messing with my barometer, I complained.

Seeing a crystal in the corner of my eye I went to reach for it, but Chorkie was there ahead of me, saying: *Mine!* When he found one that was too big for him to carry, he asked me to carry it for him, *but it's still mine*, he added.

I tried to pick it up, but couldn't lift it. The more I persevered, the more my back began to ache. *Come on*, urged Chorkie, waving a pick-axe at the horizon, *we've got all these to carry too.*

I looked around and saw great lumps of sparkling rock piled up in heaps on the hillside beside gaping holes. The needle on the barometer was bouncing up and down. I stood up, and the full horror of Chorkie's mining was revealed: mountains near and far looked like Swiss cheese. This can't be happening, I thought. And then I woke up.

My head and back both ached. I have suffered migraines for the past 30 years, so one was to be expected sooner or later. The crushing pain in my upper back was a common symptom of my AS, according to my rheumatologist, not because of a bad pitch or because I smoke. The nature of my condition is such that the pain moves around. My toes, feet or ankles might swell; my pelvic muscles might complain; the bones in my back and bum suffer on wooden dining chairs or benches; my ankle muscles strain when stepping down heavily; I get shoulder or neck pain lying on my side, upper back pain lying on my back, and lower back pain after strenuous work.

But I was also high on a mountainside, with a view of Mont Blanc out my tent flap.

So, open it, take a look, wow! Pick up the phone, switch it on, look for pharmaceuticals, melt a Zomig in my mouth for my head, check the time: 6.28 a.m., take a shot, absorb, take another shot, get out of bed, shorts on, gilet on, phone in pocket, shoes on, stretch my legs, take a pee, take another shot, walk back, pull out my toothbrush and paste, wow!

Meanwhile, no sign of life from the neighbours.

I brushed my teeth with pond water and rinsed with all but a few centilitres of drinking water. The last of that I used to wash down an Acoxxel for the inflammation. Once it kicked in, it should keep me pain-free for at least two days, even under these severe conditions. I splashed some pond water on my face, and quickly packed. My tent wasn't too damp and I could roll it up without it weighing me down too much. I wrestled my pack into place, and left, waving goodbye to the emerging Frenchmen, with  headache gone and backache easing, just after 7.00 a.m.

I must have been running on empty as I never reached Lac Blanc until after 7.45 a.m.

With the low-lying sun in my eyes, it seemed deserted at first, except at the refuge on the far side, where, as I approached, I detected the sound of low voices and morning ablutions. Some people stepped in and out of the main building, and I began to see one or two walking around the lake, or on the hillside above it.

I needed the toilet, and not just for a pee. The lack of facilities along the TMB can sometimes be a problem for those who want to leave no trace, and the volume of traffic on the trail can make it difficult to be discreet, even for a pee. Heaven knows how ladies cope, but they must, as I never caught anyone out and no one ever caught me out. But I digress.

I filled my empty plastic bottles with tap water, apparently taken

unfiltered from the lake, and went to find a place to set up the gas stove.

A leisurely breakfast in such surroundings is beyond description and I felt in no rush to move on. With the mountains, the sky, the lake and my gas stove, I was at one with the elements: earth, air, water and fire.

Some brave souls took an early morning dip on the far side, and more people came out to enjoy the tranquillity and majesty of the morning.

My schedule for the day was potentially quite gruelling and I was already behind, so I kept my appreciation of the site to one-and-a-half hours. With more time I would have climbed up the back wall of the lake and taken a look at the tarn that sits behind it, something I now regret not doing.

I wrapped up my gear, took one last visit to the refuge toilets, and set off around 9.20 a.m. Five minutes down the path I realised that I no longer had my trekking pole.

With nobody about, I took off my pack and left it out of sight behind a bush, hurrying back to retrieve the stick, which I found by the toilet door, where I had left it.

Back on the trail, with mind, body and belly recharged, I went downhill at a pace, too impatient now to take much notice of the Lacs Les Chéserys, and made good time in returning to the official TMB path at Tête aux Vents. The descent from there to Tré Le Champ is quite demanding, and probably the steepest section anywhere on the TMB. It is well-known for its vertical ladder sections and a variant can be taken to bypass them, but I had no fear of making the attempt to go down them. Chorkie steeled himself with some tea.

The further we descended, the more groups of people were coming up, most of which were willing to give way to me as a single traveller. It is customary to say *bonjour* (or *buongiorno* in Italy) to everyone one meets, though there are plenty that don't. I was passing more people coming towards me this year, thanks to my going against the flow. It can be tiresome to say hello to everyone so I start with the first and throw another at random towards the end of a group.

There were one or two sections of ladder that were a bit dicey, but for me it was mainly a question of getting my backpack in the right place so that it didn't bounce off the rock face as I descended and throw me off-balance in the process. Hence the 1000m steep descent from Lac Blanc was quite rapid, even if a little taxing on my ankles.

So many middle-aged walkers (and even younger ones) complain about going downhill for the sake of their knees, and many wear surgical supports for this reason. Despite my AS, I don't have much trouble with my knees, but my ankles are a different matter. The weight of the rucksack was putting extra strain on stiff muscles. Evidently, the anti-inflammatory hadn't reached them yet.

The TMB only skirts past the hamlet of Tré Le Champ. All I saw of it was the Auberge la Boerne, which I visited to avail myself of the toilet facilities, as well as their public litter bin. I had not been able to dispose of any waste in the last 24 hours.

A few hundred grams lighter, but more than compensated for by fresh tap water refills, I shouldered my pack and set off once again, just after midday, knowing that I was going to have to climb back up 1000m by mid-afternoon if I was to reach Refuge Les Grands, Switzerland by nightfall. Feeling the pangs of hunger again, I set myself the target of climbing 200m or so before stopping for lunch.

Fifteen minutes up the hillside at a steady snail's pace and I realised I had left my stick behind again. I was cursing the fact, when a traveller came down the hill towards me and asked if I was alright. I explained and said I had a good mind to leave it behind this time, having gone back for it once already. He insisted I would need it, and, for the sake of twenty minutes, I should dump my pack in the bushes and go back.

He made sense, so I let him pass, hid my pack and overtook him as I jogged back down the zigzag path through the forest to find the stick beside the litter bin.

When I passed him on my way back up, I wished him well and returned to my pack to find it as I left it.

Another fifteen minutes later I stopped for lunch: fried cheese and onion toastie, tea with cake and biscuits to follow.

The severity of the descent from Lac Blanc and the current climb up was having a detrimental effect on my shorts. The hem, which had begun to separate across my right knee this morning, had opened wider with each big step. The tear was now about 10cm wide. I could put a couple of stitches in it with the needle and thread I carried for just such an emergency, or I could tear it off altogether. I decided to attend to it later, and do whatever was easier at the end of the day.

A bit further up the trail, I took a breather and small-talked to some North Americans who had also stopped. They were nearing the end of their TMB, having skipped two days due to torrential rain. They'd had

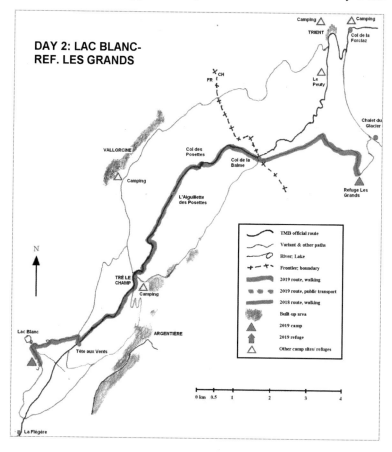

DAY 2: LAC BLANC-
REF. LES GRANDS

to get a taxi to rejoin the route at Courmayeur rather than forfeit their later refuge bookings. They had walked through Switzerland and were now planning to bypass the ladder section and head straight for Chamonix through the valley. I was very disappointed for them. They had seen the weather forecast for tomorrow and it wasn't encouraging. After their experience, they feared for me taking the Fenêtre d'Arpette variant from Les Grands tomorrow. The forecast on my phone was for some rain, but not as much as they seemed to be suggesting. Perhaps they were looking at French weather and I was looking at Swiss?

Most of the more interesting variant routes seem to go over more difficult terrains, as I learned last year, and the Fenêtre has the reputation for being one of the worst, even if one of the most visually stimulating on a clear day. Variant paths often disappear into boulder fields with only the odd painted mark to show the route across them. In France, these are short red and white parallel lines. Normally there are just enough of them if you know where to look, but if visibility is poor one can lose one's way very quickly.

I tried to put their weather warnings to the back of my mind. I still had the larger part of today's hike to complete and it was already close to 2 p.m. Any Fenêtre crossing required me to be within easy strike of it this evening, not tomorrow midmorning.

Pushing on, I arrived at L'Aiguillette des Posettes by around 4.30 p.m. and took something else to eat. This place is highlighted in the guide book for its spectacular views, as it is the highest point on the arête that runs north from Chamonix. From there, the all-round view is outstanding indeed.

I could see what I took to be the Refuge du Col de Balme marking the Swiss border 3–4km away, on about the same level, but with the Col des Posettes some 200m or so below and between.

We might reach Switzerland around 6.30 p.m., I deduced, leaving a comfortable couple of hours to get to Refuge Les Grands, weather permitting. I was about to leave when several birds of prey rose from the valley on the updrafts, like the paragliders had yesterday. Up to forty at any one time bobbed and fell, too far away for me to tell if they were buzzards or eagles and to get a clear photo.

Descending from the L'Aiguillette, the Swiss skies looked quite clear, but dark clouds were forming over the French valley behind me. It was difficult to tell if I would beat them to the border.

Some gentle rain did catch up with me on the Col des Posettes, but as I stopped to retrieve my raincoat and put it on, it too stopped. I left it on for the climb, as a cool breeze developed. By the time I arrived at the Col de Balme, which was a tougher climb than it looked from L'Aiguillette des Posettes, the wind had picked up some more, and with the sky growing darker, I wondered if I should try and camp nearby. At the top of the rise I turned my phone dark before heading across the saddle to the refuge.

A Volvo pick-up was parked outside and the front door of the refuge stood open, so I went in. Two men, one middle-aged and one much

younger, were there.

The older man was the warden and he answered my questions. They weren't officially open so I could not stop in the refuge even if I wanted to. I was welcome to camp in the fields nearby but the winds could be treacherous, and the Refuge Les Grands was only an hour or so down the path. Hard to say if it was going to rain … it was my decision.

I knew Chorkie would want me to go on. We had finally made it to the border of Switzerland and it seemed ridiculous to wait here high on an exposed hillside.

The warden agreed to sell me a can of cola and a half-litre of water (4.50€/4.50CF) and invited me to take rest in the reception area whilst he finished doing whatever he needed to do before they left on a shopping excursion. The young man stayed to keep me company.

I asked him about the path to Les Grands. After some prevarication, he admitted it was his first day here, so he knew nothing.

There was a large-scale map on the wall showing the Col and surrounding area. I checked it to see if the path to Les Grands was any easier to read. It was, and it gave me the confidence to keep going, armed with a better understanding of the lie of the land. I finished my drink and left them the can. The water went into a side pocket of my pack in case I needed it later.

Outside, the wind was still strong but there was no rain. I nipped back up to the official border post to send one last message to family, making sure I was in clear view of French receivers and not Swiss.

When I passed back in front of the refuge to take my path just after 7 p.m., the pick-up had gone. Switzerland, here we come!

The path to Refuge Les Grands started off quite innocuously. There wasn't much of interest to see as the foreground didn't fall away to reveal anything we hadn't already seen from the border. But Chorkie insisted on climbing a tree for a better look.

There were no obvious landmarks and we moved on.

Ten minutes later, I was hampered by my first (and ultimately my only) serious patch of icy snow on the TMB. Bearing in mind that the path I was following undulated around the 2200m contour of several spurs of the same 2655m mountain, I was walking with hillside above me to my right. The ice lay in a hollow with a steep drop to the left and formed an oval probably 20m across and 30m deep. At the foot of the

snow and ice, about 20m below, were a young couple with backpacks. They too were British, and were heading for the Refuge Les Grands, and, yes, this was the right path.

They warned me to take care, as the young woman had just lost her footing and hurt herself in the slide down. The footprints of previous hikers showed where I might go, but they weren't very well-defined. The only safe way to pass, they said, was to shuffle down the scree and traverse across to where they were, and do the reverse back up the other side, something I was not convinced was necessary and looked even more dangerous. I preferred to give the snow a go, knowing that, if I fell, at least I would have some company.

Treading carefully, I chopped out fresh footholds in the ice with my boots as I went, using my stick to lean into the hill side. It took time, but I made it across. The path led sharply alongside and over some rocks, but there was water pouring down it and the ground was slippy with silt. I edged round below the rocks and rejoined the path a little further on. Once there, I was able to advise the couple of their most direct route to try and rejoin the path.

They didn't seem in any hurry, so I didn't wait. For the second day in a row, I was very tired, having already been on the trail for twelve hours by this time. After two days of greeting people, I found that talking only starves one of breath. Unless I was ready to rest, I had already given up greeting those coming downhill when I was going up, restricting myself to a nod or a grunt. I certainly didn't want to get into a chatathon with my own countrymen at this stage of the day, uphill, downhill, or whatever.

When I stopped to take some photos a bit further along the trail they passed and left me behind. When I resumed walking, their lead grew, so I couldn't have kept up with them anyway.

The path wound on and on, not difficult to follow, so I was surprised to notice the couple on a different path, 100m away to my left. Perhaps they had given in and decided to find a level pitch there, I thought. I was standing by the red and white path marker so I knew I was right where I should be. They were too far away to call out to and so I carried on.

The predicted hour soon passed, but I knew I must have a good way to go yet. I was only just turning away from North-East bearing towards the South-East. As I did so, I looked North and caught a glimpse of Trient in overhead view, just as I'd seen it on the map, with the path leading up to the Col de la Forclaz clear to see.

Before very long, the path began to degrade, hidden by rivulets and disappearing across boulders. One has to step up onto them, for a little height advantage, and look around to see where the marks are before continuing. I should point out that these weren't recent rock falls. The boulders looked as permanent as any other part of the landscape.

Eventually, the Trient Glacier came into view and I knew I must be getting close. I reached the refuge just after 9 p.m.

Its warden, or volunteer guardian as I was corrected, stood outside, as if waiting for me. He said I could sleep inside for a moderate fee of 20€, or pitch up on a nice level mound a further 100m ahead down the path for free. Someone slept there last night and he had been very comfortable.

I said I had a tent, so I would like to camp outside.

He and his family were just about to light a bonfire in a hollow away from the track but equidistant from the refuge and my pitch. I was welcome to join them to help celebrate his son's nineteenth birthday. By coincidence, I said, it was my fifty-ninth birthday tomorrow.

My first priority, though, was to set up camp and get some supper. It would be getting dark in half an hour.

He pointed out an endless supply of drinking water that fed a water trough and told me I could use the refuge to make something to eat if I chose to, but to be quiet as there were (only) two other guests and they were already in bed. A small charge had to be made if I wanted to use the gas stove, but, for a few euros and a bench to sit on while the saucepan boiled, I deemed it worth it.

I set up camp quickly, re-filled my thermal rucksack with what I needed, and walked back towards the refuge. There were several people standing by the unlit fire talking French and I waved a *bon soir*.

As I sat finishing my meal, two women returned from the fire to go to bed. They spoke a little English and I a little French. I was reminded to turn all the lights out when I left, to save the battery.

When I finally made it to the camp fire, I was introduced to the guardian's two sons, the youngest whose birthday it was. Neither spoke very good English, unlike their father, so there was little more than a *bonne anniversaire* between us that didn't need translation.

The guardian explained that the 1st of August is a national holiday in Switzerland, and, as good citizens, they followed the custom of having a bonfire. He was a volunteer on duty for just a few weeks at a time, part of a mountaineering club, which may explain why the guide book suggests that the refuge is not always manned. His family was taking advantage of the opportunity to keep him company for a week. I had just met his wife and her friend.

He corrected me on my use of the name Champex, as it appears on my map and in the guide book. Champex-Lac, with a silent *x*, is the name of the town. We chatted on for some more over a drink and a smoke and I thought how wonderful to be here.

It was after 11 p.m. when I returned to my tent. Upon removing my shorts to get ready for bed, I found the right leg torn at the rear from the waistband to the hem. I wasn't prepared to use all my thread to try and repair them only for them to fail again tomorrow. They were done for, and they would be one less thing to carry, once I found another public waste bin.

My pitch wasn't perfect, but there was enough space to move around and rest my buttocks in a dip, giving full support along my back, so I slept soundly.

Chorkie ventured to sleep outside the inner tent, but under cover of the outer.

Day 3: Rain

Around 4 a.m. I was up to relieve myself. There was no moon, but the stars were as bright and plentiful as ever I'd seen them. I couldn't look down and I didn't see Chorkie among the grasses with binoculars. The thick end of the Milky Way glowed, hanging above the Glacier du Trient like its digitised reflection. Tempting as it was to stay up and keep Chorkie company, it was cold and I returned to my tent.

I slept till 6.45 a.m. and waited for a shower to pass before vacating my sleeping bag. I donned my only other pair of trousers, some lightweight hiking trousers that I had picked up from D.sports retailer for 10€, checked around that nothing had got wet during the night, and went out to freshen myself up.

Some clouds lingered. I couldn't actually see much of the Glacier du Trient from my position, but the sky above it looked clear. Whilst I waited for my saucepan of water to boil for tea, I laid out my sleeping bag inside the tent and hung my used underwear over the guy ropes to air. I had a few clothes pegs for just this purpose.

I made a cup of tea for the flask and one for myself before sitting down for crunchy muesli with milk.

I rinsed out the dishes and took out my toilet roll before walking back to the refuge to use the only proper toilet, and to ask some advice over whether or not it would be safe to cross the Fenêtre d'Arpette. After wishing me a happy birthday, the guardian reckoned it was normally doable in about six hours, so long as the weather did not deteriorate. However, low cloud was forecast, so I might not be able to enjoy the spectacular views anyway. The extensive section of rocks that I had to cross on the descent towards Champex-Lac might be slippy, and, if I did have an accident, there wouldn't be much traffic passing by that way on a day like this to lend assistance. I read that as 60/40 in favour.

I continued on towards the toilet, a one-person portaloo. The door was open towards me on my approach. Perhaps the wind, I thought, but then it suddenly slammed shut with no detectable breath of air. A few seconds later, a young woman appeared from within and explained that, seeing the door was open, I should have stood back and waited. It was to prevent a build up of bad odours. Didn't anyone tell me?

No, they hadn't. But now I knew, thank you. And off she went.

I took a seat and found another good reason to leave the door wide open: the view. I'd been paying no attention to what was behind me as I walked to the toilet and the blinkered perspective I now had only highlighted the feeling: *where did that come from?*

Out came the camera to snap shots of the glacier and the path that ran alongside and above it on the opposite side of the valley.

If I had been ready to leave at that moment I would have gone for the glacier. It looked clear to the top. But my tent still stood on the hillside and I needed to pack. Added to that, the point of no return was almost an hour's walk away. The decision couldn't be made until it had to be made.

A small beer towel is ideal for all sorts of cleaning operations whilst camping. On this occasion I used it to remove the worst of the rainwater, mud and grassy bits from the tent and ground sheet. I had to pass the water trough when I left, so I would wash it there, wring it out and hang it through a loop in my rucksack to dry.

At the trough I met a young Croatian man, presumably the partner of the young woman in the toilet. Like nearly all the Europeans (except perhaps the French and Spanish) that I've met through living and working alongside the tourism industry, he spoke good English. If I was going to Champex-Lac, he advised, I should camp at the Champex d'Arpette site, as it is hiker-friendly. The Champex-Lac site is more family/caravan oriented, and more expensive. As I would be passing the d'Arpette site on my descent from the Fenêtre d'Arpette, I should pitch my tent there and then walk down to the town for supplies. I was going to do that anyway, I thought, but I thanked him, filled two half-litre bottles for the journey, and made sure to settle with the guardian

for using the cooker before departing. He charged me a surprising 7€.

From the refuge, the sharp descent of almost 500m is on a clearly defined path through forest.

It started to rain gently on the way, and I felt the clouds closing down the pass. A few oncoming hikers were more heavily protected than I, and I feared there might be heavier showers ahead, though they didn't materialise. At the foot of the path is a sizeable river, which I crossed to reach the point of having to make a decision.

I could turn right and begin the ascent of the Fenêtre d'Arpette, or turn left along a relatively level path towards the Col de la Forclaz and return to the official TMB route. The view that I had of the glacier an hour ago was now concealed behind trees, denying me knowledge of what was happening up there. Kev Reynolds stresses that, if it looks unwise to tackle the Fenêtre, turn left.

But, how unwise was it?

If I'd been camped at Champex d'Arpette intending to cross the Fenêtre from the other side, I could have talked to others no doubt having the same concerns as I, perhaps teamed up for safety's sake. But I had chosen to go my own way, and now I didn't know what to do.

With the thundering river behind me, I stared at the signpost, as if that would help me decide.

Immediately to my right was the Chalet du Glacier, what the guide book refers to as a *buvette*, – a café for all intents and purposes. I fancied coffee and needed advice. Who better to ask than someone who works here all the time?

Chorkie stayed outside to meditate, so I took out a sweet snack, left my rucksack and trekking pole in his care, and went inside to ruminate. By enjoying coffee here, I still had a flask of tea for later.

According to the woman in charge of the Chalet, the forecast was not encouraging for the Fenêtre. The Alp Bovine side of the mountain fared better. She had no opinion on whether or not it might be safe to cross. I went outside to smoke on the matter with my companion.

Chorkie wasn't keen on getting wet. The main objective in going that way was for the views over the glacier and of the valley beyond, he reminded me. One bit of Switzerland he'd never seen before was as good as another bit of Switzerland he'd never seen before, but one bit of Switzerland he never got to see was not as good as another bit of Switzerland he did get to see.

At times like these a barometer might have come in useful, I thought. I wanted one incorporated when I last upgraded my phone, but relatively few models have them and those that do cost more than twice what I was prepared to pay. It would have been an expensive gimmick when they are available to buy as part of a multi-functional electronic compass -cum- altimeter-cum-barometer at a fraction of the difference in cost. I was only put off buying one for the extra weight of it. And I might never need it. More fool me. Would I have paid 15–20€ for some expert advice right then? Would it be worth another hundred grams in my pack? Probably, but I had to work this one out for myself.

On one hand, it was my birthday and I wanted to do something special. This pass

is 2665m asml, equal to the Col des Fours that I crossed last year. Together they are the highest passes on TMB official variants, the top and tail of the Mont Blanc massif, so it would be a shame not to bag the pair. Normally, crossing a boulder field would not be a problem for me, and my ankles were feeling a little stronger this morning.

On the other hand, perhaps this was one of those questions of knowing my limits.

When I thought about how my predicted timings for each day were so far panning out, there was cause for concern. I had estimated three hours walking on my first day and I was actually six hours on the trail, admittedly in no hurry, but falling short of my target. Yesterday I was on the trail for thirteen-and-a-half hours instead of seven-and-a-half (including the previous day's shortfall). If my estimate for today was six-and-a-half hours, then it could easily take me eleven. I left the refuge this morning at 9 a.m., so that could mean arriving at the camp site after 8 p.m., hungry and short of food supplies.

Furthermore, it seemed the chances of fine weather were low, while the risk of some bad weather was high. Any bad weather could add considerable chunks of time to my day and add cold and wet to hungry.

I wasn't willing to allow my determination to push me beyond my physical limits today, and Chorkie had a point: we would play it safe and rejoin the standard TMB route. I turned left.

The path from the Chalet to the Col de la Forclaz is evidently popular with the locals, many walking dogs. There is a section where the path has fallen away from the hillside and some ingenious carpentry has restored it via a 10m section of cantilevered walkway, complete with handrail. From it one gets an excellent view of Trient. It added an extra perspective to the map-like view I had of it yesterday, and helped to build the bigger picture of the TMB in my mind's eye.

Despite having to double back to some extent this morning, yesterday's walk along the contours to Les Grands had saved me an 870m descent from the Col de la Balme to Le Peuty, where bivouac

camping is permitted, and another 50m descent into Trient before climbing 250m back up to the Col de la Forclaz, with an official campsite nearby. I took consolation from the fact that I had not wasted so much breath climbing back up again.

As it came to me, the Col de la Forclaz is on a short section of the TMB where it coincides with a main road. There was a mini-supermarket-cum-tourist shop, so I stepped in to idly look around, leaving my rucksack by the door. I was struck by a large display of souvenir stuffed toys. Chorkie had started 'life' like this.

When my children left home several years ago, I was left with bagfuls of cuddly toys of this kind to throw out. What happens to all these gifts that people bring back from their holidays, I wondered. How many of these St Bernards, cows, teddies and marmots will be cherished in any way, and how many will simply go in a cupboard or on a shelf to gather dust?

Heartbreaking, not just for the sentimentality, but for the waste.

Do we buy them, either for ourselves or as gifts, to assuage the guilt we feel for the harm mankind has done to animalkind? Is there a correlation between cruelty towards animals and the rate at which stuffed toys are manufactured and sold?

I think the shop attendant must have noticed me motionless in reverie, for she stood up from her chair on the far side of the shop to peer across the shelving, and asked if she could help. I said I was looking for clothes.

There were jackets, poles and small accessories of all sorts but there were no shorts. There was no point to buying groceries here, so I picked up my rucksack and went outside. As I did so, it struck me that I had no trekking pole. I couldn't see it outside the shop, so I must have left it at the Chalet du Glacier, fifty minutes' walk back. Was it an excuse to buy some groceries and return for an assault on the Fenêtre d'Arpette? Or should I leave it behind and manage without?

I rummaged in my rucksack for the tattered remains of my shorts and threw them (and other accumulated waste) in the public litter bin whilst I had the chance, some 350-400g, taking it down to around 16kg, I guessed. I took a drink and biscuit – I needed to think again. No wonder it took me so long to get through the day.

Carrying two poles on last year's TMB attempt had been frustrating. When I wanted to stop to take a photo, which was quite often, it meant un-looping the strap of at least one and finding somewhere to put it/them before fetching out my camera. (To make matters worse, I carried a compact camera with a good optical zoom as well as my phone with a more-limited camera for snapshots.) I would poke the poles in the ground to free up my hand(s) completely, but on rocks that isn't practical. Even on earthy terrain, they don't always stay where you put them, and on a slope there is a risk they can skitter away. So I tried passing the loose stick to my other hand, or slipping it under my arm, or sliding my hand straight through the loop to let it dangle, but none of these solutions were practical or comfortable.

When in use, they often got trapped between rocks as I moved forward, and I was constantly resizing them depending whether going uphill or down. To make matters worse, I was looking down at where the tips were landing more than I was looking at the scenery.

After four days of misuse and abuse, one pole jammed tight and refused to telescope shut. So, when I returned home, I researched the pros and cons of trekking poles on the internet. I watched videos showing the correct way to use them to save energy, and to transfer weight from the knees to the upper body. These were their primary benefits, apparently. However, the people demonstrating them were always on well-made straight paths, a rarity on mountain passes, so that made me wonder.

The things that I found irksome were among the commonly quoted cons, as was the suggestion that their use exaggerates the damage done to the footpath by ramblers and hikers. So it was also an environmental issue, and perhaps another one of those marketing ploys to make you think you need something when you really don't.

There was nothing as scientific in favour of using one stick (and certainly no marketing of same), but I found a video of an elderly gent whose anecdotal evidence was in favour of one.

So I decided not to replace them, and to manage with just one, to see what happened. As soon as I made that decision, I felt the pressure of unwanted advice diminishing.

Until now, the only nuisance one stick had caused me was having to run back and forth to pick it up from where I'd left it. It had proved helpful on yesterday's traverse across the snow.

But, meanwhile, I had been managing quite well for fifty minutes on the flat with no poles. Going up or down hill might be different, but the fact that this was the third incidence of my leaving it behind in two days was the clincher. My subconscious was trying to tell me to give it up, to leave it for some other poor soul to get the benefit of it if they needed it, as it wasn't for me. Any energy I saved by using poles was being wasted every time I stopped, even without having to retrace my steps. And my knees were fine.

I headed for the Alp Bovine feeling even more relieved of the burden. *Now I've seen*, I said to myself.

Despite Chorkie's excitement, and my own, at being in Switzerland, the day's walk turned out to be underwhelming.

Climbing gently from the Col de la Forclaz, we eventually caught glimpses of the valley beyond the TMB. Throughout France, I had walked the hills parallel to the massif, with my attention drawn towards it. In Switzerland, I was crossing the northernmost part of the massif itself, looking outwards. The first part of yesterday evening's walk from the Col de Balme to Refuge Les Grands was stunning, and seeing the tiny village of Trient this morning from above brought it to life like one of Hermann Hesse's sketches. But that was still within the boundaries of the TMB.

Now I had returned to the boundary trail and it had been only forty-eight hours since I left civilisation, but the neatly laid out houses and roads of Martigny looked alien and invasive.

A little over halfway to the Col we heard our first Swiss cowbells and passed close beside their source. Separated by a cable fence, the open field was a good place to sit on a rock for a smoke, a drink, and to commune with the cows. Heavy cloud smothered the mountain between us and the Glacier du Trient. A couple of farm buildings stood nearby but we were alone for a few minutes until a large group of TMBers appeared from the forest ahead.

The low cloud and an occasional drizzle provided the perfect balance of temperatures between warming humidity and cooling spots of rain. There was no need to take shelter and no need for a raincoat.

At the Collet Portalo (2040m amsl), the highest point on today's trail, there were twenty-plus hikers, in four or five huddles of from two to ten, with more heading up the trail towards me in twos and threes. I set up to prepare some tea and some lunch on a flat rock just below the crowds, and, when I looked behind me again, I was alone. The newcomers that arrived didn't linger, so I took my photos and enjoyed the vistas in peace. No one came up the hill from behind as I had done.

Puffy white clouds shrouded the mountain tops, but the path ahead

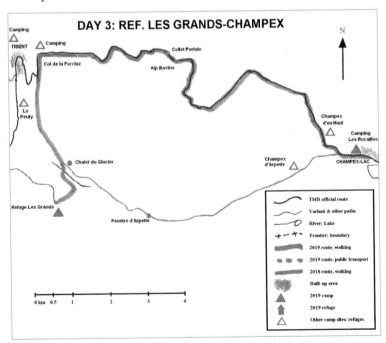

looked free from rain. The Fenêtre d'Arpette was obscured by the hillside to my right, but the heavier clouds I saw earlier had lifted a little. Judging by the traffic I had met so far, there couldn't have been many crossing by the glacier that day.

Less than ten minutes into a gentle descent I arrived at the Alp Bovine itself, where accommodation and refreshments are available. With its proximity to the high point on this stage of the TMB, I'm guessing it's popular with those that dine out rather than carry food. It was certainly busy today.

We enjoyed a pleasant, though uneventful, afternoon's walk and arrived at Les Rocailles camp site, Champex-Lac (approx. 1450m amsl), some time after 5 p.m.

It is, as I had been warned, a busy site full of vehicles and big tents, and I was horrified to learn the cost of a pitch was 16CF/16€. But I was in no mood to backtrack 2km to the Croatian-recommended site and there was free wi-fi here, so I would be able to talk to my family on my birthday without incurring high roaming charges. I paid in Swiss Francs, as they are technically worth less than Euros.

A supermarket was available about 1km down the road, but due to close in 30 minutes. It was a good thing that I wasn't counting on going there after coming over the Fenêtre d'Arpette. There wasn't time to pitch my tent, so I left my pack outside reception and made it down there without delay.

I was tempted to buy something special for my dinner, but a half dozen free range eggs cost 4.50CF, and a punnet of strawberries cost in excess of 6CF, reflecting the fact that food is comparatively expensive in Switzerland. I really fancied an omelette for supper, so I bought the eggs, but left the strawberries. I wasn't in the mood to celebrate anyway.

I found a half litre of C.cola for 1.50€, only 0.15€ more than in my local supermarket back home in Spain, and a half-litre of full cream UHT milk for less than 1€, so not everything is ridiculously expensive.

When I went to leave I realised I had nothing to carry my shopping in. I asked for a bag and was refused. The checkout girl intimated, in French, that I was welcome to help myself to a fold-up plastic basket. I pointed out that they were closing and so I couldn't return it tonight. No problem – *à demain*. Very trusting, thought I, this would not work in the UK or Spain.

I returned to the camp site, picked up my pack from reception and sought out the area assigned to small tents. I found a nice-looking space and put down my pack to stake my claim. Off came the boots and socks, to free my feet for scanning the grass for bumps and pebbles – I wanted an undisturbed night.

Without rushing I had the tent erected in less than ten minutes. As soon as everything was in its proper place for the rest of my stay at Champex-Lac, I took my towel and soaps for a shower.

I remembered to ask for the wi-fi code before returning to the tent. An email from E.lines had arrived, stating that they would arrange for a partial refund.

Feeling so much fresher and healthier, I cooked myself a delicious omelette with onions and cheese as part of a four-course meal.

By the time I had spoken to different members of my family, it was getting dark, so I settled in for the night whilst Chorkie posted updates. He slept inside this time.

Day 4: Lake, Tree, Mountain

After scheduling three difficult days, the fourth would be my first chance to relax a little. My destination was only 15km away, with a gentle descent to Issert (1055m amsl) to begin with, and a gentle ascent to Le Fouly (1610m amsl), through what promised to be pastoral Switzerland. On paper, it's easy to see why Kev Reynolds, and others, suggest that Champex is the ideal place to begin the TMB clockwise.

The weather forecast was good, so after an uneventful breakfast I packed away. Not so much dew this morning.

I returned to the supermarket with the basket just before 9 a.m., backtracked to an unmarked path, and took the long way around the lake, to avoid some of the main road.

Champex-Lac has a chocolate box charm, and the attention to neatness and tidiness that Switzerland is renowned for. Old men fishing and mothers with pushchairs added to the idyll. No backpackers other than myself. I'm glad I took the long way round on this occasion.

Just after rejoining the TMB on the main road at the far end of the lake, the path turns hard right down a gentle hill onto the Sentier des Champignons (Mushroom Trail) and into forest.

I took my time along its course for there are many wooden carvings of forest animals, some quite menacing to Chorkie.

On arrival at a clearing with several paths apparently leading away from it, I looked for the familiar mark of red and white and saw a

yellow diamond with a black outline. They have something similar in Italy, I recalled. Odd, though, that there were red and white marks on the path to Refuge Les Grands, so I couldn't be sure when these diamonds started. There was a picnic table and I took the opportunity to enjoy a second breakfast of tea and biscuits.

I am reminded that my ability to describe landscape and things is limited, so anything I could say about this countryside walk would fall short. Prior to Hermann Hesse, the nearest thing to poetry that I read came from the inside of a record sleeve, by the likes of Peter Gabriel or Patti Smith. It would take one of the great poets to do this place justice.

All I can say is that for an hour or so I was happy to be *Wandering along the mountain track, with a knapsack on my back.*

Hermann Hesse may be better known for his novels, like *Steppenwolf*, the story of a middle-aged man who discovers the man inside the wolf, or *Demian*, the story of a boy who discovers the angel inside the demon. But one of his better-known lyrics, *Trees*, appears in

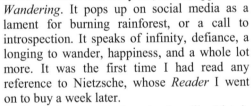

Wandering. It pops up on social media as a lament for burning rainforest, or a call to introspection. It speaks of infinity, defiance, a longing to wander, happiness, and a whole lot more. It was the first time I had read any reference to Nietzsche, whose *Reader* I went on to buy a week later.

That led me onto other classics, like Plato's *Republic*. The famous analogy of the shadows on the cave wall caused by the flickering light of fire, which the captive cave dwellers take to be a representation of truth, is still relevant today. In place of fire, modern mankind has the light of the television, the rhythm of the music and the heroic feats of sporting celebrities to captivate and distract them from what is really going on around them.

In the same book, using Socrates as his mouthpiece, Plato also considers the creation of an ideal society built on justice. His plan seems practical and will serve the people's needs until one of his audience of wealthy citizens objects, saying that if this is to be a happy city, then there should be some measure of luxury beyond mere subsistence. To accommodate this criticism Socrates introduces the need for an army, so that the city may seize more land as the population grows, and to defend itself from potential invaders. The logical extension over time is all-out war.

Modern democracy is allegedly indebted to this book, but the clear causality of war as a consequence of unlimited economic growth seems lost on all but a few modern political philosophers. We now face the accumulation of many years' over-stretching the confines of what the planet can sustain and the emphasis is still on how to get more bang for the buck, never accepting that the problem is more deep rooted.

There is nothing new under the sun, only different characters in different places refracting and reflecting the same patterns over and over.

I wondered if Chorkie is a shadow on my cave wall, or a prism through which I might refract my experiences into words.

We rejoined the main Champex-Le Fouly road at the lowest point above sea level on the Swiss section of our Tour (Issert, 1055m amsl), followed it south for 100m, and crossed to a parallel path on the other side of the road. A stretch of worn asphalt led uphill to a loose string of mostly old wooden houses, many in poor repair. This must have been the hamlet of Les Arlaches (1117m amsl), though I saw no sign. Cars stood idly by, no noise emanated from anywhere.

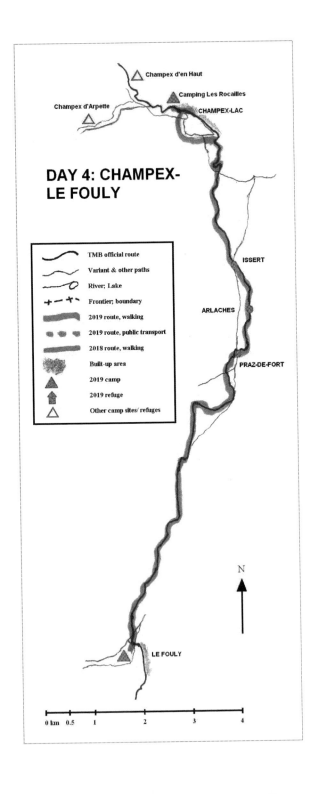

DAY 4: CHAMPEX-LE FOULY

Champex d'en Haut

Camping Les Rocailles

Champex d'Arpette

CHAMPEX-LAC

	TMB official route
	Variant & other paths
	River; Lake
	Frontier; boundary
	2019 route, walking
	2019 route, public transport
	2018 route, walking
	Built-up area
	2019 camp
	2019 refuge
	Other camp sites/ refuges

ISSERT

ARLACHES

PRAZ-DE-FORT

N

LE FOULY

0 km 0.5 1 2 3 4

The road was devoid of life except for the floral displays. Aside from the neat stacks of firewood everywhere, it was hard to believe that the houses might be occupied. It felt like a ghost town, until we happened upon some garden gnomes. Chorkie got himself acquainted and I waited to hear what they had to say.

Tez Satterday arter holdy Thezdy, and they Swizz they tooked to gallyvanting, zee, he told me.

Wood is clearly the fuel of choice in these parts, and its stacking seems to be a matter of pride, for it should be deemed an art form. Sometimes firewood is as much a part of the fabric of the building as the balcony or walls.

Further on, *For Sale* signs appeared at several properties. With all the tourists passing by, I shouldn't have thought that they would be for sale for long. But the fact that they are for sale is perhaps in indication that it is not so easy to live here as the countryside is idyllic.

Other than walkers on intersecting paths, not a soul did I meet for an hour. When walking between two places like Champex and Le Fouly,

with no hostelries or camp sites between them, and no obvious variant route, the popularity of the anti-clockwise trek over the clockwise becomes more obvious. I had the trail to myself all morning, stopping and starting. It was only just before Praz de Fort that I began to meet oncoming TMBers.

Beyond Praz de Fort, Chorkie went in search of salmon whilst I bathed my feet in the fast flowing river. I examined them for blisters and swelling and was pleased to find none so far. There was no rush so, a hundred metres on, I collapsed on a bench in the shade of an old tree to prepare my lunch of hard-boiled eggs, tomatoes and bread.

The trail between Issert and all the way to Le Fouly is largely along well-made footpaths, dirt roads or asphalt, with a moderate gradient. A couple of steep, but short, sections of climbing through forest paths made me gasp for breath, with my heart at its limit and I began to wonder if I was ever going to feel fitter. *Quit smoking*, said a voice, probably my GP's.

I was able to keep an eye on the unfolding scenery as it opened up behind, a pleasure which I suspect is heightened when entering it from the other direction. For me, I was walking uphill and the walls were

closing in. From the other direction I would be entering a new land, slowly opening its doors and revealing its mysteries, so it depends which way you look at it.

I arrived at the foot of Camping Les Glaciers camp site before 4 p.m. and turned off the TMB path into it. It took me ten minutes to find my way through. It is close to 1km from end to end, full of tents, campervans, caravans, glampers, chalets and more, of all shapes and sizes. Peak holiday season.

I stopped at a toilet block en route and noticed an abundance of power points there, some of which were occupied with mobile phones.

At reception, I joined a short queue of people and was eventually attended to by a young man. I tried my French to ask for a one-man tent, one night.

He out-Frenched me, saying *Tour du Mont Blanc?* so that it sounded like three words, which threw me off-guard. I said: *Yes, is that a problem?*

Oh no, it's just for the paperwork, he reassured me, in French. A long list of other personal details had to be taken, and the price came to 16CF/15€. I made sure to get the wi-fi code, to save me coming back, and paid in Euros, saving my remaining 20CF to restock on food and drink.

I was shown a map and directed to the TMB zone, three ten-by-ten-metre mini-zones partitioned by bushes, shrubs and the like. They were more or less in a line beside the river, just beyond the toilet and wash block I'd visited earlier.

The first zone was already full of tents, so I headed for the unpopulated lower section, beside a community room, furthest from the toilets. I don't like a long walk to have a pee, but neither did I want to be so close I could hear everyone going in and out all night. I was still less than 25m away.

I found a flat and grassy area beside a bush that I could drape some clothes over, or run a guy rope to at a pinch, carefully laid the ground sheet out and set the tent up. Emptying out everything else I might need, I took my half-empty battery pack to the toilet block, to put it on charge before all the remaining power points were nabbed, before doing anything else.

Then off to the C.chain village supermarket for some basics. I know others might come here for fondues or other Swiss delicacies, but I just wanted carbs, the sweeter the better. Having been brought up in 60's and 70's Britain I could not resist the temptation to buy a bumper-size Swiss roll filled with cream and a little jam.

I had a shower, washed my undies in the wash room, and went back to enjoy the view over dinner. The camp site is in a spectacular location and the mountains that form the natural boundary between Switzerland and Italy are quite breathtaking. Switzerland, Italy and France come

together at the peak of Mont Dolent (3820m amsl), an eye magnet for anyone staying on the camp site. Chorkie and I sat hypnotised by the light cutting across the clouds, as the sun dipped behind the mountains alongside Mont Dolent. Better than any firework display.

There was still plenty of daylight left to attend to my trousers. With only two days wear, the waistband had lost its elasticity. The weight of my phone in the side pocket, and the dampness caused by sweating thighs, had dragged them down, to the point where they were hanging off my bum, as seems to be the fashion among young men these days. But clearly these young men don't do much walking, because, for me, the sensation was very uncomfortable.

I thought about cutting the legs down to convert them into ragged shorts. But I couldn't be sure if I would need long trousers later on, if it turned cold. I'm not a fan of belts at the best of times, nor of elastic waistbands. My size and weight have barely changed in forty years so I normally buy clothes that fit well. But these trousers were cheap and lightweight, so one can't have everything.

I fetched out my first aid kit for the needle and thread and made a few stitches to bunch the waistband between belt hooks, reducing it by a couple of centimetres. I tried them on and they were good to go.

My step-father, F., would have approved of this solution. He worked his way up to dairy management from humble beginnings, but remained very careful with his money. He never threw anything away if he could repair, remodel or repurpose it, which made for some interesting and ingenious fixes around the house, using leather, scrap metal or salvaged wood.

He was a good father to me, and an all-round family man, with a witty remark for every occasion. One of his first duties as my legal parent was to attend my school careers night. Without knowing why, I felt drawn towards design-based work, but I had no achievement in that field. My instincts weren't encouraged, however, so I stayed on to follow an education ideal for business. Meanwhile, F. fed me one part-time job after another, which gave me a broad range of work experience and made a man of me in terms of body strength.

At University, I began to question the assumptions of Economics: that human behaviour can be quantified mathematically, with its primary goal as the maximisation of consumption; that there exist finite resources from which to make goods; and that specialization and the division of labour is fundamental to the efficient production of goods.

Greed is not a given whilst concepts like love, sharing and kindness exist. Humans may be limited by life span, by ability and by physical constraints, but nature exhibits infinite variety, with every creature, plant and snowflake unique. The goods essential to life are limited in number at any given moment, but they are infinitely reproducible. Even manufactured luxury goods may be recycled to some extent. And, given the adaptability of humans to different situations, specialization pigeonholes and dehumanizes workers, limiting their potential.

So I rejected business, and bought an expensive pair of walking boots to go my own way. Thirty-six years later, shortly after F. died, I went camping alone for the first time and discovered they were no longer waterproof. For want of time and money to replace them, and perhaps in honour of F., I repaired the collars with leather patches for last year's TMB. They served well, so they're getting one last outing this year.

But sometimes, you have to know when to throw something away. This was my fourth night out and I hadn't yet used any of the four nightlights infused with mosquito repellent oil. (I also carried some citronella-infused joss sticks for repellent.) They could obviously be used for light too, but my USB-chargeable head lamp provided all I needed. They might serve for autumnal evenings, but I was carrying them for nothing now, so I left them by the waste-bins, saving 44g of excess baggage, the same weight as Chorkie, I thought, malevolently.

Saying nothing, he went to bed early, inside the tent, and I went for a walk around the site before my final visit to the toilets. Whilst there, I realised my shampoo and shower gels weren't among my toiletries. I checked the shower I'd used, just in case, but there was no trace.

My battery was less than 80% full. Undaunted at the apparent theft of my shampoo, I left it there overnight. I would need to recharge my phone from it tomorrow.

Day 5: Mountain Pass

Sure enough, I needed the toilet during the night and had the presence of mind to check my battery again. It was fully charged, so I took it while I remembered and went back to bed.

It was 6.25 a.m. when daylight woke me and I opened the tent flap to look outside. Mont Dolent was tinged a rusty red. Over breakfast, the shadow crept down the mountainside and the tinge became a wash. This was a much more interesting start to the day than yesterday.

Today I would be heading 1000m up to cross into Italy. The guidebook profile shows the recommended route to have an average gradient similar to yesterday's climb, though twice the length. Heading out of civilisation, I hoped for less well-made tracks and more wide-open countryside views of Switzerland.

From the border, I would begin covering the same ground as I had on my previous attempt on the TMB, so over breakfast I revisited an alternative route that I had noticed before leaving home.

The standard route passes to the left-hand side (east) of the Tête de Ferret, via the Gran Col Ferret (2537m amsl) and descends at a moderate rate into the Italian Val Ferret.

The alternative is shorter, going directly through the Swiss Val Ferret to the west of the Tête, crossing the border at the Petit Col Ferret (2490m amsl), 40m below its big brother. The walk up from either side to the Petit Col is much more severe, particularly from the Italian side,

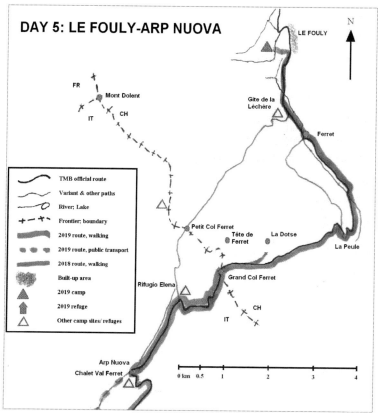

DAY 5: LE FOULY-ARP NUOVA

LE FOULY

N

FR

Mont Dolent

IT   CH

Gîte de la Léchère

Ferret

TMB official route

Variant & other paths

River; Lake

Frontier; boundary

2019 route, walking

2019 route, public transport

2018 route, walking

Built-up area

2019 camp

2019 refuge

Other camp sites/ refuges

Petit Col Ferret

Tête de Ferret   La Dotse

La Peule

Rifugio Elena

Grand Col Ferret

CH

IT

Arp Nuova
Chalet Val Ferret

0 km 0.5   1   2   3   4

and, of course, most trekkers come from Italy into Switzerland, not the reverse as I would be doing, so I suspected it is not a particularly popular route.

I had considered this crossing as a potential short-cut in case I was delayed in getting to Champex. (By continuing on from Le Fouly last night, I might have reached the Petit Col by 7 p.m.) A further 300m of elevation and 1–2km alongside the arête towards Mont Dolent is a place marked suitable for bivouac camping. Staying there, I could have descended to the Val Ferret in the morning and caught up on the lost day by continuing straight on to tomorrow's agenda.

But I wasn't sure there was any point in going now. I wanted to cross as many of the highest points on the tour as possible, preferring to go high at the expense of low. As of today, I had yet to reach 2500m amsl. The Gran Col Ferret should have been the second of six 2500m+ passes (after the Fenêtre d'Arpette) and the Petit Col was sub 2500m, even if only by 10m. And there was a consolation prize on offer near to the Grand Col … I would make the decision on the trail.

The colours of the mountains toned down over breakfast, but the sun still hadn't risen enough to flood the camp site directly. It prevented my tent from drying out.

I don't carry scales around with me, but, due to the large surface area of a tent and groundsheet, it's not unreasonable to suppose that a heavy dew can add several hundred grams to its weight. I dried what I could with my beer towel, but yesterday's washed underwear hanging on the guy ropes overnight hadn't dried, so that was another couple of hundred grams to carry.

I couldn't wait for the sun to show up, and left the site just before 9 a.m. The hills had turned green, the rocks were grey and the glacier had returned to white.

I stopped at the same supermarket before leaving the village to use up my Swiss Francs. A ready-made cheese sandwich, a banana and a bottle of C.cola almost cleared me out. With the remaining 25 cents I tried to buy six grapes on a small vine, but they came to 28 cents, so I was asked to return one. I didn't think I could get away with stripping the grapes from the vine and leaving that behind, so I popped one in my mouth and walked round the shop. If I hadn't then it would probably be neglected and thrown out at the end of the day.

The Petit Col Ferret route involved taking a right-hand turn not far out of Le Fouly, at or near a turning to the Gîte de la Léchère. It came sooner than I expected and there was no mention of the Petit Col, so I moved on, expecting to see another path. I should have taken out my map and guide book to check, but I didn't. The path didn't materialise, and, by the time I realised, it was too late to retrace my steps. Perhaps because of an unconscious reticence to take the steeper climb, I found myself remaining on the standard path towards the Grand Col. A couple of kilometres further on, there was another choice to make, according

to the guide book: one can choose to stay west of the river and take the rugged path through trees, or to cross the river and pass through the village of Ferret onto 2km of gently inclined road east of the river before climbing on a footpath to rejoin the western route again. I couldn't find the rugged path, so this time I did take out the map and guide book. The map shows the path, but not as an official variant.

With no sign of the alternative route on the ground, I crossed the bridge to the village. The hamlet seemed quite sizeable, and there is allegedly a hotel here, but I saw no sign of commerce.

Beyond it, the path rises then dips back down to the river before crossing back on to the western bank. From the bridge I espied a good-sized log stripped clean of bark beside the river, the perfect spot to take a second breakfast, to bathe my feet, and to lay out my underwear and unroll my tent in the warming sun.

The hillside path allegedly rejoins the main path a couple of kilometres further on, near the Gîte Alpage de la Peule (2071m amsl), the last recognised place to stop overnight in Switzerland, but I can't say that I noticed any signpost. I suspect the route fell into disuse between the publication of my 2015 Cicerone guide and the publication of the map (2018), possibly as a means to protect the hillside forest from the erosion of ever-increasing traffic on the TMB.

La Peule consists of five conjoined bungalows backed into the hillside, each one housing its own purpose: toilets, an unmarked door, a work/craft shop, a bar, and finally a fast food joint. Perhaps the *gîte* was well-disguised but I could see no indication that accommodation was available, unless it was through the unmarked door. Large containers filled with colourful flowers stood either side of the path. Further on, in the path and overlooking the valley, some café tables and chairs were shaded by parasols and populated with clientele. Beyond them were a couple of large tents, presumably yurts. It all looked quite charming and very inviting.

I asked at the fast food joint for a fresh water tap. They offered me bottled water, I said no, *free* water. And, with a look that said we don't

do anything for free here, was sent back to the toilet block. Not all tap water is recommended safe to drink, but there is usually a small sign to say whether it is or not. There was none, so I filled two half-litre bottles, enough for tea and to splash around my head and face. On my way back up I noticed the *No Picnic* signs which made it clear that only paying guests were welcome!

Beginning to think about lunch now that I had water for tea, I kept on going through the mostly grassy green but plain scenery, preferring to stop in a more secluded spot anyway.

There were some more walkers on the path going the same way, and I wondered if they were day-trippers from Italy on their way back in or day-trippers from Switzerland on their way out.

I noticed the tendency I have, after rest, of setting off at the fastest pace I can manage, until my breathing gets deeper to compensate for an excited heart, and I have to stop. That's what I did here, gasping after about 200m on a gentle gradient.

If I was having trouble taking in enough oxygen, then it stood to reason that I was not giving what I took in the chance to soak in. By holding my breath five seconds or so, I could make two or three steps uphill on a full tank, so to speak, and not keep the heart waiting for fresh air. I tried it, as tempting as it was to breathe out and back in again, and it seemed to help.

I have only ever been hospitalised twice, both times for a chronic nose bleed. On the first occasion, my wife was one day overdue with our second child. I'd been bleeding on and off for most of the past twenty-four hours when I was finally admitted for hospital treatment. They packed my nose with cocaine-soaked bandages, gave me a dose of morphine and kept me in overnight. Next day, my wife was admitted to the maternity ward and I couldn't be with her, confined to bed at the other end of the hospital. The bleeding never stopped, so, five days later, they broke my nose, drilled my nostrils out, and inserted splints until it all healed. They called it an SMR. I called it the worst eight days of my life.

The second, identical, operation came less than three years later. It cost me another week in hospital. This time, however, it left me able to breathe through both nostrils for the first time in my life.

I read up on breathing exercises, particularly those recommended by Hindu yogis. All my life I had been led to believe that I should breathe in through my nose and out through my mouth. Throughout my teenage and adult life until then, I suffered badly with catarrh, throat infections and coughs. I had a double dose of pneumonia in between nose bleeds. Now I was reading that one should breathe both in and out through the nose.

It made sense: the nostril hairs capture the dust and foreign matter as it goes in, and the exhalation of breath blows it back out, keeping the nasal passages free and clear. It becomes more difficult when exercising because there is a tendency to draw great gulps through the mouth, particularly if one's nose is partially blocked. But one has to persevere until it becomes second nature. Breathing heavily through the mouth in rarefied mountain air might be understandable, but, in cities and near industry or roads, it is a recipe for infection and/or illness.

Since I adopted this method, I stopped suffering from annual infections or bronchial problems. If I detect a sore throat coming on, I eat an orange or two and the irritation goes.

Re-training my breathing was keeping me going further each time before having to stop. I forgot about food and began to think about the consolation prize for coming the long way round.

At around 2400m amsl, according to the guide book, there is an unsigned (but apparently well-worn) path which forms a fork with the path I was approaching on. It makes a ten-minute detour, still east of the Tête de Ferret, but to the smaller peak of La Dotse from where there is the promise of excellent views. I just had to keep my wits about me and hope the unmarked trail was still clearly defined after the recent thawing of winter snow.

Finding it turned out to be easy enough. As my altimeter climbed through 2390m amsl, I saw an almost parallel path above me ten paces to my right and traced it to its source with my eyes, to be sure it did in fact meet the path ahead. I tiptoed through the long grass and wild flowers to cut the corner and turned right towards La Dotse.

Other walkers were ignoring it as they came down the hill, so perhaps it would be easier to find a quiet spot for lunch. Half way to the summit, I found myself overlooking the Swiss Val Ferret, a magnificent view denied to those that go via the Grand Col and stay on the official path. And there was no one else there.

I went closer to the edge where there is a small cairn beside some flat rocks and Chorkie immediately claimed it. It was the perfect spot for

lunch, and Chorkie could not agree more. This was the best view of Switzerland we'd had, with Le Fouly and the low point of Issert (where we first entered the valley) both visible. Champex-Lac was not to be seen, however, it being tucked into the hillside left of Issert as we viewed it. It was another section of the 3-D map engrained in my head.

Perhaps these and other features would not have been so apparent if we were going anti-clockwise, but, putting myself in those shoes, it certainly did offer the hiker a land full of promise.

Eventually, a small group came up the path towards us, but they carried on past to the summit of La Dotse. I wondered if I should have gone that little bit further.

The only advantage they gained is a better view of the valley we just came through, assured Chorkie, from the top of the world.

Fifteen minutes after returning to the path we arrived at the Grand Col Ferret.

When I had reached the Grand Col from the Italian side, cloud obscured both sides, an anti-climax after so much expectation at reaching Switzerland. A few trekkers excitedly took photos of each other, and marshals stood shivering, waiting. As I went to leave, the leading half-UTMB contestant appeared out of the mist, topped the Col, and disappeared once again into the mist. One by one, more runners came past me as I descended, and the cloud began to lift to reveal magnificent views and hundreds, if not thousands, of competitors running uphill towards me, spread over three kilometres below. They had all left Courmayeur at 9 a.m. for the race to Chamonix. I was in the

race track, going against the flow, a very odd sensation. It was probably this that inspired me to come back for another go at the Tour.

But no UTMB runners this time – they wouldn't be here for another three weeks.

The weather was perfect and we enjoyed a good half hour soaking up the more elevated views over Italy, listening to the distant but calming clang of cow bells, and recognising the smell of cow shit that wafted up from below. The only cows we had seen, or cow bells we had heard, through Switzerland, were between Col de la Forclaz and Alp Bovine.

The picture perfect Matterhorn could not distract me from the subtle restrictions of that apparently highly-controlled and clockwork society, which lifted inexplicably when I returned my gaze towards Italy, with

its rather more laid back approach.

The signpost predicted a 1h 40mins walk to Arp Nuova. I wanted to catch the 17.43 bus from there and the time was approaching 4 p.m., so I got up to leave.

After almost five days on the trail my ankles had gained strength enough to bound down the hillside where the path was clear. The descent was just as breathtaking this time as the first, a year ago. Now and then it felt like free falling.

I overtook what few were going in the same direction, and stopped frequently to take photos or to let climbers pass without forcing them to lose their rhythm. I was in high spirits and felt in excellent health. This was what it's all about.

Looking behind me and to my right, I glanced across towards the Petit Col Ferret and Mont Dolent. Clearly the path down from it would have been quite severe, though, of course, it always looks worse from below than it actually is.

I stopped half way down the descent for a little refreshment in the

shade at Rifugio Elena, and reached the Chalet Val Ferret and the bus stop at Arp Nuova with two minutes to spare.

Non-camping TMBers might have stopped at the Rifugio Elena, at the Chalet Val Ferret, or continued on from there towards Rifugio Bonatti, another 250m up and 5km along into the hills south of the Val Ferret. But I was camping, and all the official Italian camp sites lie close to the rivers in one or the other valley either side of Courmayeur.

Having spent three nights there the previous year and enjoyed my stay, I intended to catch the bus to Courmayeur and onwards to Hobo Camping in the Val Veny. This being a Sunday, I wasn't expecting to find any shops open in the town, so had stocked up in Le Fouly, and the camp site has its own small shop for any emergency items.

A one-way ticket through either valley costs 2€, but for only 3.50€ one can travel on all the local buses all day. Asking for *tutto il giorno* in crude Italian is crucial, otherwise the driver pumps out a ticket for one journey without being asked.

I took further advantage of my prior knowledge of Courmayeur by leaving the bus before it reached the town. Had I gone to the terminal, the wait for the Val Veny bus is around 50 minutes. All the local buses leave the town on the same road heading towards the Mont Blanc tunnel at Entrèves. A small C.chain supermarket (open!) stands alongside the shared bus stop where the routes converge. I disembarked there, crossed the road, and the Val Veny bus came within seconds.

Hobo Camping, since 2016 (Camping Val Veny Cuignon on my online map), has its own bus stop, only 250m beyond another bus stop and camp site (Campeggio Aiguille-Noire), where I noticed a couple of backpackers disembarking.

Beyond Hobo, the bus goes another 2km to Visaille, where it turns

round and heads back. Restricted traffic only is permitted to pass Visaille and enter the nature reserve beyond, with 3km of asphalt before the main TMB route is rejoined at Lago Combal.

Camping prices at Hobo had shot up. No longer under 10€, each night would cost me 14.20€. Perhaps they now had more facilities? I provisionally reserved for two nights, instead of the three that I had originally intended to, for reasons I would evaluate on the morrow.

I was directed to a plot, not far from where I had pitched the year before, by a young man whom I had not seen last year. In fact, the presence of extra staff was the only improvement I noticed to justify the price-hike.

Barefoot, I pitched my tent to the sound of The Doors playing *Weird Scenes Inside the Goldmine* over the camp p.a. They were still being *weird* when I came back from my soap-free shower in fresh clothes. The couple who had left the bus at the earlier camp site had arrived and were pitching their tent nearby. I suspect they found the Aiguille-Noire site rather more geared towards glampers and caravans, whereas Hobo Camping bills itself as *The Last Resort*.

There is a kitchen for campers, close to where I pitched, ideal for when your supplies of camping gas are running low. The site attracts its own share of campervans and caravans, as well as family-size tents, so one might have expected the kitchen to be overrun, but I had no trouble getting access to rustle up the rest of the eggs in an omelette.

The free wi-fi helped again, though I had more than enough free roaming available if necessary. Chorkie uploaded his King-of-the-Swiss-cairn photo.

My trousers had held up well today and I went to sleep satisfied, knowing that tomorrow promised to offer the highlight of highlights.

Day 6: Glorious World

The weather forecast for today and tomorrow was good as far as tomorrow evening (Tuesday), when rain was threatened. That much had not changed since it first appeared on the week-to-view online forecast. But the forecast for Wednesday morning had deteriorated from *showery* to *downpours*.

Over breakfast cereal, and another anti-inflammatory, I mulled over my options: whether to stay Tuesday night at Hobo and make my way to the French border and the pre-booked Refuge Robert Blanc for Wednesday as first planned, thereby risking a wet night on Tuesday and a good soaking on Wednesday; or to steal a march on the bad weather and book into Rifugio Elisabetta, for a 3km walk beyond the Val Veny asphalt, keeping my kit completely dry on Tuesday night and slashing my time on the trail through Wednesday's rain. The extra expense would be in the region of 25–50€, depending on the cost of the refuge. Few refuges accept credit cards, because of their remoteness from the network, and I realised my mistake in paying cash for the first day's expenses. If I were to pay for a night at Elisabetta, I would leave Robert Blanc with next to no cash, and have to wait till the following evening to acquire some.

The second option looked favourable nonetheless. I owed it to myself to keep as dry as possible. I've had pneumonia twice before, and my wife, who understands these things, is always telling me a third time could be fatal. I don't know about that, but I don't fancy it again, whatever. It would mean either: doing Tuesday's allotted walk without my backpack and returning to Hobo early in the afternoon to collect it; or to leave Hobo on Tuesday morning with my pack, lug it over the mountains, and go straight on to the refuge, saving myself the extra 6km of walking in total.

The first decision was best made today, as refuges can easily be booked up 24 hours in advance. The second decision could wait depending on how I felt tomorrow morning.

I left my tent, my large rucksack and most of my belongings behind and packed my small thermal rucksack with my flask, my valuables and some snacks.

I bought a ticket for *tutto il giorno* and rode all the way to Courmayeur bus station this time, to pick up the next bus to Val Ferret. They leave half-hourly, and I would have gained nothing by switching at the supermarket, but I still had time for a cappuccino and brioche at the station café. At 2.70€, it was cheaper than any coffee and pastry I'd had elsewhere, and both tasted spectacular. I took the opportunity to snaffle a few sachets of sugar for my dwindling supplies and went out to wait for my bus.

I still had five minutes, so I phoned Rifugio Elisabetta in case they shut up shop for the morning. A man answered in English, putting paid to my fears it would be answered in Italian. They could accommodate me at 45€ for half board in a dormitory. That was near the low end of my expected price range, so I reserved a place. It was worth 30.80€ extra for the hot food and for the peace of mind that I wouldn't have to carry a wet tent into France. He asked me to try to arrive by 6 p.m. for dinner at 6.45 p.m. I felt confident about arriving on time, so long as the rain didn't come early.

That resolved, the bus came and I was able to enjoy the journey. I disembarked at Arp Nuova just before 10 a.m.

In *Wandering* [*Farm*], Hermann Hesse tells of his arrival in the southern foothills of the Swiss Alps, and how it feels like he is coming home from banishment. The people and buildings seem to be a world apart from those he left behind. He has reached some kind of sanctuary from the madness. I recognised that feeling when I stopped here briefly. It did feel like coming home, I could sit anywhere I pleased and feel comfortable. With tears of joy welling in my eyes came tears of sadness that I was leaving again so soon, two days running.

This stage of the TMB is replete with alternative routes. Aside from the bad weather option of walking the length of the Val Ferret, mostly on the only road, to Courmayeur, there are two-and-a-half alternatives.

Last summer I had left Courmayeur and walked the standard route up to Rifugio Bertone (1989m amsl), a climb through forest of around 750m with limited views, before following the main route between the 1900–2050m contours to Rifugio Bonatti (2025m amsl) and beyond, with some more undulations before a steep descent to Arp Nuova at 1784m amsl. That in itself was perhaps the most spectacular day on my first visit here, but I was determined not to repeat myself where other options existed.

From my current perspective, the two Mont de la Saxe part-variants begin as one, diverging from the standard route at Rifugio Bonatti, climbing to over 2524m amsl at the Pas-Entre-Deux-Sants, before descending and rising to 2426m amsl at the Col Sapin. At this point they split, with the longest and highest option rising up to the Tête de la Tronche peak at 2584m, continuing along a high ridge before finally descending to rejoin the main path at Rifugio Bertone; the Val Sapin option is more direct, cutting out the high ridge, with a winding but steady descent down the valley, rejoining the main path 1–2km below Rifugio Bertone. I preferred the high ridge option.

The descent from Rifugio Bertone would have to be down the same

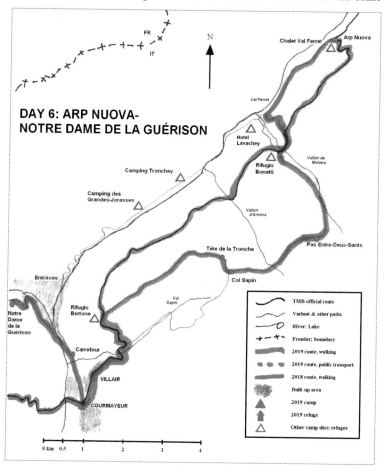

DAY 6: ARP NUOVA-
NOTRE DAME DE LA GUÉRISON

forested path to Courmayeur as last summer's climb to it, but I could jog it like a trail runner without the encumbrance of a heavy backpack. Even if my heart still suffered on the climbs, my ankles had proven in good shape for descending yesterday.

Prior to all that, however, I had to get to Rifugio Bonatti. Rather than take the steep ascent to the 1900m contour on the official path, I chose to walk 3km along the Val Ferret road to just before Hotel Levachey, losing height at first, with the intention of cutting up through the trees and emerging just below the refuge.

There are very few buildings and the road is mostly deserted due to restricted access. Ordinary traffic is turned back alongside Hotel Levachey, where there is a nature resort popular with day-trippers and other visitors by car, not unlike that at the far end of Val Veny.

Last year, after my aborted trip to Switzerland, I walked a kilometre or two alongside the river, but it was tough going among the bushes and trees, with no path. Neither photos nor video can do it justice because the sound of the river, the freshness of the air, and the sensation of belonging cannot be faithfully captured. The road veers away from the river somewhat but offers stunning views along the valley and within it.

I turned up towards Rifugio Bonatti, along a winding forested path, with ever-widening views across the valley. It wasn't anything like as spectacular as the main TMB path, but, without walking it, I would never have known. No doubt it had been quieter than the main route, with the majority pouring out of Rifugio Bonatti and heading on towards Arp Nuova on the standard route.

Being low on supplies, I stopped at the refuge to buy a cheese sandwich (6€) for later, to use their toilet and make use of the terrace to soak up the views of the mountains opposite with tea and a cigarette.

Leaving the refuge, and departing from the main path, the Vallon de Malatra looks like an empty glacial basin and the path turns right towards the saddle of Pas-Entre-Deux-Sants, temporarily obscuring the

mountains on the far side of the valley. Up here the Tour markings can be little more than a yellow blob of paint on a rock.

I was astonished to see a couple of mountain bike riders pushing or carrying their machines over the worst patches of terrain, and I easily overtook them. They overtook me near the top of the Pas, as I stopped to admire the view over the Vallon d'Armina. The absence of any sign of civilisation highlights the sense of wilderness, with barely a soul in sight. It was an ideal place to finish my flask of tea and eat some sugary snacks.

It was only when I reached the river passing through the bottom of the basin (2285m amsl) that I realised how truly big the landscape is. On the hillside ahead the mountain bikers were barely discernible.

Mont Blanc should have been visible, but proved shy once again, hiding behind cloud. In its absence, Chorkie recreated Balmat's first ascent, superimposing himself at 4810m amsl. He returned the favour for me, with my head at about the level of the bivouac site on Mont Dolent

The climb wasn't too arduous but it took time. At the Col Sapin, a mother with small children sat in a camping chair. Was she some guardian spirit of the mountain, or just a dutiful wife waiting for her husband to return from his climb? I didn't ask.

The perilous ascent to Tête de la Tronche is steep and uneven, and either side of the path I was aware of a severe drop. Sufferers of vertigo beware. And yet, I swear I saw someone carrying a

pushbike up ahead of me. Courmayeur came into view, more than one vertical kilometre below, as I climbed away from the Col, sometimes on all fours.

I pitied the poor devils with heavy packs and trekking poles coming down from the Tête. They looked ready to fall at any moment and I sensed fear in the eyes of more than one. I had only my two-year-old cheap trainers underfoot, rather than walking boots, and I began to wonder if that had been a good idea. But they had done me proud last summer, and they did once again. I made it to the summit to witness something unforgettable.

The entire 10km-wide Italian wall of the Mont Blanc massif is on view, an expanse of rock and glaciers laid out in a long line about 4km

away. I managed to capture it in a panoramic shot, with the Col de la Seigne the lowest point on the horizon to my left and the Cols Ferret the lowest on my right.

Ten to fifteen minutes alone there is humbling. One could forget all one's cares, until someone else arrives to spoil the moment.

Descending gently along the ridge parallel to the Val Ferret below, the view keeps on giving for several kilometres. Once again I was almost in tears and I broke into song: ... *with a knapsack on my back.*

After passing through a huge flock of sheep, goats and cows tended by a shepherd, I set my pack down and looked back to where we had come from.

The Cols Ferret formed the lowest points on the far horizon, with the 4208m Grandes Jorasses dwarfing Mont Dolent to their left, and a line of 3000m+ hills to their right. We had barely scraped the sides of either.

Chorkie hailed a sheep, which approached, so I stood back to give them space for a bear to baa chat. I have no idea how they communicated but they parted with a kiss – an authentic David Attenbearough moment.

A little further on, our passing disturbed some birds of prey and we were once again treated to a short aerial display, though too far away

this time to capture any definition on camera.

Eventually, the path drops away and veers left to merge with the standard route at Rifugio Bertone. Two ponies in the field above the refuge approached the fence as I did, hoping for treats, but I had none to offer and they backed off. In the background, Mont Chétif (2343m amsl) dominates the view.

From the refuge, the 750m of steep descent is mostly through forest with some fine views over Courmayeur. It took me just over an hour as I bounded down it and passed through Villair, a village on the outer environs of the town.

Entering the town of Courmayeur beside the church and the *Società della Guide* (guide's office), I walked round the corner and into a mountaineering/sports shop. My trousers were dragging down once again and I really wanted some shorts for the daytime.

Upon asking an assistant for help, in Spanish, she responded in English, offering me a pair that seemed to be suitable but I was taken aback by the price: 115€.

That's more than I would spend on an entire wardrobe, I protested. *Are there any cheaper?*

They had a bright green pair with a white stripe, reduced to 89€.

No thanks, I said. *I'm not Italian enough to get away with those*, and changed tack. I asked about C.gas, (in the blue cylinders) which I was running low on, or small gas burners.

No C.gas, but they had two different models of burners, similar in design to mine. At 32€, the cheaper one was clunkier and heavier, requiring a range of gas I'd seen elsewhere. The 40€ model was lighter and more elegant, but I didn't recognise the required gas brand and it wasn't cheap. The assistant assured me it was widely available, but I refused to be backed into a purchase there and then.

The issue with my current burner was that it had suffered the wear and tear of time and use. I found it among some books that I bought twenty years ago, when I had the shop in England, apparently brand new. Since then it has travelled with my wife and me to many places and boiled many a pot of tea. It had long ago lost its ability to self-spark, but, more recently, one of the tines had misaligned. Good balance demanded that I rely on two level tines, rather than three with the pan on a tilt. I had tightened a hard-to-reach nut inside it six months ago, and that helped, but it had worked loose again.

I could replace it with an identical model for 20–25€ back home and know that the gas is widely available, but it would mean making do for now. In the shop, I was tempted by the more expensive model, but thanked the good lady and said I might be back tomorrow.

I fancied an ice cream, but, when I thought about paying 3–4€ for a scoop from one of Courmayeur's high-priced outlets, it made no sense. I would be happy with a family block for half the price. I marched through the town centre without stopping again and continued along the bus route towards Entrèves, leaving the TMB official route behind.

I needed something filling for supper, two days' supply of snacks, perhaps some sandwich fillers, and some milk. The C.chain supermarket was just along the road.

C.cola was only 1€ for a 660ml bottle, so that was a must! I needed shampoo/shower gel but it aggrieved me that the smallest bottle weighed 200g, as I had no intention of taking it home with me. But I wasn't willing to go another week without a decent wash.

There wasn't much fresh meat left: two packs of steak, some chicken fillet, duck breast, liver, pork chops, and a few other things I didn't recognise. There was a huge chunk of minced beef which might do for a burger. I had a look in the freezer compartment. I looked at the cheeses, and considered eggs, before returning to the meat. The chicken and pork were gone and the only thing left that appealed to me was steak. I had to make a quick decision if I wasn't going to be left with vegan burgers. The cheapest of two packs cost 7.50€: a bit extravagant, but I had my birthday disappointment to make up for and today was worthy of celebration. I grabbed it before someone else did. I kept looking and found some milk, but there was no fresh bread left.

I found a litre tub of ice cream for 2€. After paying, I sat outside and tucked into it with my teaspoon, devouring almost half.

I packed away my purchases and walked on, turning left. The road is not busy, essentially a no-through road, running towards the French border. The walk is not without interest, as it first crosses the river just below where the two valley rivers meet, then rises up the south bank of the Val Veny, overlooking Entrèves and the tunnel entrance before turning hard left to follow the valley floor. Just before the bend is the Notre-Dame de la Guérison church. It was closed (at 6 p.m.), so I could not enter for any divine inspiration, but I would return tomorrow. I finished what I could of the ice cream whilst I waited for my bus, and dumped the melting remainder in the litter bin when it arrived.

The little camp shop closed at 7.30 p.m. and I just missed it, but the bar was quiet, so the young woman led me through the back and into the shop. They had bread rolls, as well as C.gas in my size, which I took the opportunity to buy, as well as some locally-made cheese.

I tracked down the Italian manageress and asked about the laundry service. No problem, she said, it takes about three hours and its 5€ for the wash, 5€ for drying. That was twice last year's price, but it was worth it if I didn't have to dry everything on a line. I gave her all the clothes I wasn't wearing, as well as my towel (after showering), and she said I could empty the dryer in the morning.

I prepared cheese-steak sandwiches in the kitchen to more sounds of the sixties and sat on the comfy furniture outside to soak up the evening. A fire was lit in front of the bar, as it was the night before, and when I returned to my tent I realised that I would not be going back to buy a new gas stove in the morning.

I added a 2cm pleat to the other side of my trouser waistband to hitch them up again, and prepared for bed early.

As I lay back, reviewing today's photographs, I noticed Chorkie nodding along in the screen light to *On The Road Again*. It's our song, he said, referring to Conkers: *dum-de dum-de dum-de dum-de, duh-duh-dum* …

Day 7: Chapel

I slept through till nearly 7 a.m. and went directly to use the toilet. On my way back I stopped in to pick up my clothes from the dryer. Yesterday's glorious sense of freedom convinced me to enjoy another day without my backpack. A dry start to the day meant I could pack everything away promptly, and appeal to the manageress to stash my gear till later. Once again, she was very accommodating. I settled my bill and said I would probably be back by lunchtime.

The standard TMB path leaves the *Società della Guide* office in Courmayeur, descends through the town, passes by the bus station, and crosses the combined rivers from the two valleys beside the main road, to rise up through the enchanting village of Dolonne. From memory, the climb to the Col Chécrouit is quite steep through a pleasant forest with limited views, but the Col itself has some splendid views. From there the balcony path follows the high-sided walls of the line of hills running parallel to the south-eastern side of the Mont Blanc massif. Col Chécrouit forms an apron of land between Mont Chétif (2343m), the conical hill on the edge of Courmayeur, and today's route. The gap marked by the descent from Rifugio Bertone and the climb to Col Chécrouit is what allows the waters of the rivers to evacuate through the Aosta valley, and motorised transport easy access from the south (from Italy) to the foot of Monte Bianco and Courmayeur. Without the tunnel providing a short-cut to Northern Europe, Courmayeur would be at the mouth of a T-shaped cul-de-sac. I had entered at the top right tip of the *T*, and was exiting at the top left.

For now, I intended to reach Col Chécrouit from the other side of Mont Chétif. Paying for *tutto il giorno* again, a short bus ride took me to the Santuario de Notre-Dame de la Guérison before opening time.

I have no truck with any authoritarian religion, but I am curious about the siting of churches, chapels and all places of pilgrimage. Very often

they are built on former pagan sites of worship, and very often such sites are reputed to have healing energies. Megalithic sites, such as stone circles and standing stones, are numerous across the UK, and all around the world. But, to my knowledge, there are no recognised sites in and around the Mont Blanc massif.

A devoted Christian, with whom I had many a discussion over builder's tea, once advised me that water divining, or any kind of dowsing, is considered witchcraft by his church, an offshoot of the Church of England.

A few years later, a man who claimed to be able to dowse became a regular visitor to my bookshop. Whenever he sensed energy he tingled all over, he said. And he could map dowse with his fingers. I was sceptical, but he occasionally bought books, so I humoured him until he stood in front of the counter one day and said: *There's bad energy here.* I thought I'd insulted him, but no, he was talking about the place where he stood, not me.

A few days later, a frozen pipe burst directly above where my customer had stood. Coincidence? Witchcraft? I don't know. On the bright side, I was well-insured and it gave me a good excuse to completely redecorate. He went on to identify other invisible phenomena, so I began to take an interest in this aspect of the supernatural, which seemed to have some substance.

It stands to reason that the Church of Rome would have suppressed any sites of pagan worship within Italy, before all else, and rewritten history through the building of churches in sacred places, thereby limiting access to any potential beneficial earth energies, real or superstitious.

The fact that the walls of the current sanctuary built on this site (in 1867) are partially-covered with crutches left here by pilgrims may be a clue to the healing nature of the place, though it is officially attributed to the miracle of the statue.

It was a shame that it was not open, but I was too impatient to wait. Retracing the road I had just ridden along, it bears left into the Val Veny proper. The valley waters come thundering down a steep decline as they take on water from the Glacier de la Brenva, and are multiplied again as they go down past the tunnel entrance, like some cauldron for negative ions. If it feels this good here, what might it be like in the Sanctuary?

1km further on, at Plan Ponquet (bus stop 47), I forked left towards the Rifugio Monte Bianco on a road with restricted access. As it passes the refuge it forks again.

The right hand path follows the same contour, passing behind the camp sites, and rejoins the road close to the final bus stop at Visaille. It forms the bad weather alternative to today's climb to the Mont Favre

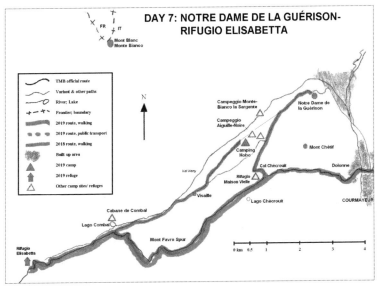

DAY 7: NOTRE DAME DE LA GUÉRISON-RIFUGIO ELISABETTA

Spur. By the time I went back to retrieve my backpack later this day, I would have walked all but 2km of it.

The left hand path serves as a ski run in the winter and leads to the Col Chécroit by a different path to the one I descended last year. For second time in two days I had taken a less-interesting route to the standard path. But if one doesn't try them, one never knows.

Climbing away from the Col, with its bare landscape and open views, one enters trees and begins to pass the small art installations that pepper the track over the course of the first 2km. A series of *alternative views*, some using mirrors, highlight some of the details on the opposing mountainside which might otherwise go unnoticed.

Lago Chécrouit is a natural installation however, a small pool set back in the hillside. I'd wanted to get there whilst the track was still

quiet and I made it by 10.45 a.m. It is well worth the effort to walk around, as, from its other side, a perfect mirror image of the mountains opposite is revealed that can take the breath away.

The low cloud obscured the skies rather more than I remembered from my last visit, but added their own drama. I had the lake to myself for five minutes, until some walkers arrived from the opposite direction with a dog. One threw a stick in the lake, the dog dutifully followed it and shattered the mirror.

I took second breakfast and tried to relax as I waited for the ripples to subside, irked by the irresponsible stick thrower.

I was never fond of dogs. In fact, as a child, I was uncomfortable around all animals, particularly those with wet snouts or fleshy tails.

Nor could I accept the idea of eating fleshy foods, and an irrational fear of eating in public meant that I couldn't face school dinners. My mother was obliged to make arrangements for me to walk home (a mile each way) for lunch. When weekly visits to the municipal swimming pool began lunch breaks were shorter, so special provision had to be made for me to take in a packed lunch. Nowadays, it seems every child has a packed lunch and most of them are fussy eaters.

My elder brother was at times a great companion, at others mean and spiteful. That added to my seclusion, which increased after my father died.

I always had a scientific mind, trying to find causal links between apparently unrelated things, attempting to make sense of the world for myself. Accelerated by my brother's influence, I became cynical of most children's media long before I ought to. The first feature film I saw, on its release, was *Mary Poppins*. I was enjoying it until the cartoon segments began and trashed any suspension of disbelief. I was taken to see *The Sound of Music, Oliver!* and *Chitty Chitty Bang Bang*, by which time my patience for musicals, or any fantastical story involving children I could not relate to, was expended. The reality of the death of my father hardened me against any film or story where a principal character (usually the father) dies at the beginning, only to miraculously reappear for the happy ever after finale. A fondness for the mock-realism of puppetry (as embodied in, for example, *Thunderbirds* or Rod Hull's *Emu*), was the only childish notion I carried through.

On my eighteenth birthday I started a summer job as a milkman. Making door-to-door deliveries brought me into close contact with dogs on a daily basis and, armed with the right to be on their property as well as my growing level of strength and fitness, I overcame my fears. I still didn't like them much, but over time, I realised that it was the attitude of the owners that irked me more than the dogs themselves.

My diet widened and my understanding of the world increased, largely thanks to B. We shared the same flat in what became the squat across from my favourite bookshop. He was a plasterer and an artist, twelve years my senior, and recently separated from his wife, so our backgrounds were very different. But we were both at a crossroads in our respective lives, and he developed my taste for wild camping. According to his interpretation of American Indian history and the influence of something other than just beer, we became blood brothers.

I interpreted my rejection of economics as some kind of Nietzschean metamorphosis from camel to lion, and B. showed me the beauty in nature, as the lion gave way to the child. I recognised the importance of all flora and fauna, each with its own unique characteristic, acting as part of the planet's own checks and balances – a revolting slug serves its purpose, and I even learned to like some dogs.

The tendency for nature to be anarchic may be all that prevents us from indebtedness to mechanization and orderliness. Extreme weather and the melting of the glaciers and polar ice caps are evidence of the earth's thermostat reacting to mankind's frenetic overactivity. As sea levels rise it might force us to higher land, and to reconsider the contradictions of expecting unlimited growth from a world of limited resources. Earth might sustain us a good while longer if we weren't so eager to consume it before someone else does.

Mankind has been fighting among itself and ruthlessly abusing nature for millennia, sterilising wildlife and the land, replacing what was once freely available with synthetic alternatives and calling it progress. The march towards a vegan food diet to protect animal life seems laudable, but I cannot get past the irony of replicating meat products with heavily-processed vegetable protein. It has taken almost one hundred years for mankind to realise the damage being done by plastics, so by the time we come to our senses over the homogenization of all other things natural, it may be too late.

Vegans suggest that a plant-based diet can help minimise the effects of climate change, but eating some meat as part of a varied diet seems to keep me relatively healthy. A little of anything in moderation can do no harm and one should not be ostracized for that while there are some that eat meat with every meal, others go starving, and vast amounts of all kind of foodstuffs are wasted by industry and householders daily.

And, yet, here I am on tour with a synthetic anthropomorphism of one of nature's greatest creatures. But Chorkie is lighter to carry than the tripod that I would need for delayed-action shots of myself looking epic, and he keeps a straight face: poser.

Using a tiny model in a gigantic landscape, without special effects, is also a challenge. I can't control the camera settings very well, so I trust the camera to do all the work, whilst I do my best to take advantage of what it offers, finding some interesting composition to fill the screen. And puppets offer the puppeteer the freedom to challenge the boundaries of *normal* behaviour, and to do so with a humour that appeals across the age spectrum.

If there is a serious side, then it is that I am infinite in relation to Chorkie: he is inanimate without my perception and interpretation. He represents a facet of my psyche, just as I might represent a facet of what is infinite to me. He is a shadow on my cave wall, as I am a shadow on the wall of my infinite.

As humans, we each see a different facet of the same infinite: some believe in gods; some imagine a computer simulation with themselves as programs; some see a Universe of random atoms animated by electro-chemical impulses; and so on. Any religious leader, philosopher or scientist that pretends to define the infinite is a liar, for any finite definition is a simplification, otherwise it would not be infinite.

What matters, on a day-to.day basis, is what is in one's heart. All one's morals, ethics and willingness to take responsibility for one's actions derive from the infinite. Everyone has a unique view, so ultimately, one can choose to be self-centered, willing to trample over others, and greedy for the fruits of the earth, or one can choose to be respectful of all living creatures and planet earth as a whole. Anything in between exposes us to hypocrisy.

I packed up, took a few more photos and moved on to enjoy the overhead views of Val Veny.

The path rises and undulates, with splendid views of the mountains and glaciers across the other side of the valley, as well as into the valley itself. It finally peaks at 2430m amsl on the Mont Favre Spur, an

excellent spot for lunch with views across to the Glacier du Miage and others, with the Val Ferret now far behind us.

From the spur, the path descends quickly towards the milky waters of Lago Combal: not so much a lake but the intersection of multiple tributaries given to flooding. The Cabane de Combal stands across the other side at a safe height – a pretty spot to spend the night, no doubt.

The TMB officially turns left past the lake and rises slowly on a

passable road, most of the way to the Rifugio Elisabetta. But I had to go back for my pack first, so I turned right and entered the asphalted road towards Visaille. The descent to the bus stop is close to 450m, through a nature reserve. Once again, the river gave off an invigorating energy.

I missed the hourly Visaille-Courmayeur bus by 15 minutes and realised it would be quicker to keep walking the almost 2km and be done with it.

It was a tiring drag through the hottest part of the day, and I was ready for a cool drink at the Hobo bar.

I caught the bus back to Visaille and, by the time I arrived at the lake to resume my Tour, three hours had passed. The morning's walk to that point had taken less than five hours, so, ultimately, I am not sure if I saved any energy by not carrying my pack all day. But saving energy isn't everything: it had been another spectacular day, and I was done with what-ifs. I was still gambling on there being rain bad enough to make it worth paying to sleep indoors.

Once off the asphalt, the earthen road continues for a couple of kilometres without a noticeable gradient, periodically crossing babbling rivers.

A short sharp climb precedes arrival at some abandoned and derelict military barracks, just before a turning to the refuge. From below, it looks to be very exposed. The signed path to the refuge spiralled around from the front to the back, where hand-made signs led me full circle to arrive at the front door.

Dark clouds over France had begun blocking out the sun, but there was still no sign of rain as I entered into a busy boot room at 6 p.m.

Several people were sitting, some milling about. I asked for reception, and someone pointed me through a door. Another reminded me to change my boots for crocs. Heaven forbid, a new experience for me.

As I complied, I realised how quiet it was, and turned round to note that everyone was looking at a phone. Is this the wi-fi zone, perchance?

The warden was from Argentina and he had a team of young Spanish-speaking volunteers to help with the chores. His English was perfect so I persuaded him to stick with that and I checked in for a dormitory room of twenty-four. He tried to upgrade me to a four-person dormitory, for just 10€ extra, but I was sceptical.

One of the volunteers led me to the dormitory to show me bed five, on the highest of three platforms each sleeping eight. The ceiling would prevent me being able to sit up in bed, but at least it should be dry. He insisted on showing me the smaller dorm too, in case I wanted to upgrade, then left me to make my own mind up.

I went back to the big dormitory and took out only what I needed from my pack. Chorkie had been sleeping inside the tent at camp sites, and now he stayed in his pouch, untrusting of other people. A found a vacant space on the floor to stand mine among all the other rucksacks, and returned to the reception area.

I ordered a packed lunch for tomorrow at 10€, but turned down the 10€ upgrade. Paying 2€ for a shower token, I used the excess of hot water to wash the day's t-shirt, underpants and socks in some shower soap underfoot, and nipped outside to hang them out on one of the many washing lines above the refuge.

With ten minutes to spare before dinner, I headed for the door to the balcony overlooking the Val Veny to enjoy a smoke. My guide book states that the sunsets from this refuge can be out of this world, though it wouldn't be due for a couple of hours yet. Before I reached the door, however, the bell rang for dinner and I turned back to find my table and beat the rush.

The refuge was quite full, with groups of all sizes and nationalities. To avoid confusion, the staff had allocated tables. I found my name on one with eight others and went to slot myself into the bench seats. A middle-aged woman sat by the window on my side, and a middle-aged man faced her. He stretched out his hand and introduced himself by name straight away. I reciprocated, and did the same to his partner. He and I immediately struck up a rapport, as he guessed I was a builder of some sort, and he laid wooden floors. I recognised his accent as Kiwi. He was touring with his English wife, who was as quiet as he was talkative.

A group of six young women joined us to complete the table, and it turned out they were from New Zealand too. Engrossed in conversation, I lost track of time and the sky began to darken. When the first course, of risotto, eventually came, it lacked seasoning and it seemed there was only one salt pot for the entire room.

A light rain began to fall.

As the plates were cleared away, the chatter on my table continued, but in waiting for the second course, I came to my senses and went outside for that smoke. My washing would be getting an extra rinse but there was nothing to be done about it now. Perhaps the morning would be dry and bright after all.

I took a couple of photos, and it soon became apparent that I wasn't going to get a very good picture. This was a new phone and I hadn't learned to make best use of the settings hidden behind tiny icons that I couldn't see without my glasses on. I used to have such sharp vision, until I reached the age of fifty. Never let it be taken for granted.

I couldn't pick up a phone signal, never mind wi-fi, so gave up with the tech and went back indoors.

The main course consisted of pork, beans and potatoes, which I enjoyed immensely, and the dessert was a panna cotta.

By the time it was over, it was nearly 8.30 p.m., and a storm had developed. I went out for another smoke, sheltering under the canopy. A middle-aged woman from Barcelona sat there smoking. She knew my town well. She and her husband were walking from refuge to refuge, anti-clockwise, having done the route clockwise on a previous holiday. We conversed in Spanish, comparing notes as long as I could bear the splashes.

The boot room was still full of people making voice and video calls, but I couldn't connect for a weather update. I wrote a couple of messages to my family, added a photo of the rain, and sent them without knowing when they might be received.

There wasn't much else to do, so I was in bed by lights out at 10 p.m. I expected to be woken frequently, but, apart from my need to use the loo in the night, I slept as well as ever.

Day 8: Rainy Weather

Wednesday began dry, overcast with a glimpse of sunshine towards Courmayeur, and heavy cloud threatening the Col de la Seigne and France. I washed, dressed, and went outside to check my clothes. They were soaking wet, so I wrung them out and re-hung them in the hope they might dry off a little more.

The clouds lifted over breakfast and the mood was upbeat, with everyone nervously hoping for a fine day's walk despite all forecasts. The middle-aged couple were heading for Le Peule, Switzerland, equivalent to two-and-a-half stages. They were travelling light, but, still, it was a helluva hike. I gave them the benefit of my recent experience, and suggested they might want to stop short of the border, particularly with the bad weather forecast. The girls were only going as far as Courmayeur. I was going solo in the opposite direction, so we wished one another good luck and went our separate ways.

I spoke to the warden about the prospect of crossing directly from the Col de la Seigne on the IT-FR border along the alternative path towards Refuge Robert Blanc, my one pre-booked refuge. He strongly advised against it – it was for experienced mountaineers only – and suggested that I descend to the Refuge des Mottets (1870m amsl) on the TMB official path and take the gentler route up to Robert Blanc (2750m amsl) from there.

But that's almost 900m of climbing, I protested, instead of 250m direct.

The path is easy down to Refuge des Mottets, he said, and the upwards path to Robert Blanc is for tourists and much quicker and easier than the more direct route from the Col, which would be flooded with overnight rain. I might have to walk further, but it would take me no longer, and be a lot safer.

It wasn't what I wanted to hear.

There was still no phone signal, inside or outside, so I gathered my clothes, finished my packing and went out on the veranda for a last look at the sky. It didn't look bad. The Kiwi girls were there taking photos of one another under the Glacier de le Lée Blanche. I offered to take a group photo for them and they returned the favour. We wished one another good luck again and I left.

No sooner had I rejoined the trail than I saw some marmots ahead of me and to the right of the path. I stopped to take photos and discovered that my camera wasn't so good at long-range zoom shots either, or perhaps I wasn't using it right. I couldn't get a clear image and I couldn't approach any closer without scaring them away.

Walking on, within five minutes, the clouds shed their load and I ran towards some rocks that might provide temporary shelter. They didn't offer much and I wondered about running back to the refuge, but the rain grew heavier and I saw the chance to squeeze under the biggest rock through a gap barely big enough for me. The rucksack could stay outside, with my ground sheet over it to keep the worst of the rain off.

There was still no phone signal, and I waited, expecting the rain to stop quickly. Ten minutes in and I was beginning to feel the cold and realised I should put some extra layers on, a task which was made difficult by the cramped space I had taken cover in. Chorkie climbed out to stretch his legs for the first time since last night. I had to hunker down a little further when the rain grew heavier, but he had plenty of headroom.

A half-hour past, and I heard voices. Peeking out, some hikers in ponchos passed by, heading towards Courmayeur. They looked drenched and I remained where I was.

Some more people passed and I thought the rain might have stopped. I readied myself to climb out, but changed my mind when lightning struck somewhere across the border and the storm picked up again. Chorkie was getting bored and returned to hibernation, leaving me alone with my thoughts, which began to turn dark.

I was sheltering among a pile of rocks that may have fallen or washed down the mountainside in relatively recent times – nature had not yet carpeted them all with earth and grass. They looked stable enough when I climbed in among them, but, who knew what it might take to unsettle them? Was I reckless to trust my life to them staying put?

I once thought that my Dad was reckless to do some of the things he did. He would ask someone to hang onto his belt whilst he leaned out over a cliff face to take a photo; he would volunteer to be the last in a line of fifty to risk being jumped over by some daredevil on a flying motor cycle; he was actually prosecuted for dangerous driving; and he died crossing a main road in dark clothes without street lights, hit by a car driven without lights.

If not reckless, perhaps he was fearless, trusting others with his life too freely.

He was the disciplinarian, my mother soft on me. He was always quite practical and he taught me a few carpentry skills, which I never pursued at the time. I don't recall him ever getting on his hands and knees and playing with my brother and I. He was a keen scout in his youth, and volunteered to my local cub scout group to encourage me to go, but I was a bit of a wimp, and after a few months I quit.

He was a toolmaker by trade, so he and my step-father were both good craftsman in their preferred medium, my father with metal, my step-father with wood and leather. My father was disciplined and serious, my step-father more flexible and jovial. But my father was a shop steward, my step-father a boss; my father was the wild man, my step-father the wise; my father smoked a pipe, my step-father never smoked; they both loved travel, but my father loved camping, and my step-father loved the sea. Though I had tried to find my own way, to find my own interests, my choices in life have been influenced by both in almost equal measure.

The rain eventually stopped and the clouds seemed to part a little.

It took me five minutes to extricate myself from the hole and climb back down with all my gear to the ground. I had spent almost an hour-and-a-half there, but at least I was still dry, with the rucksack cover in place and my raincoat on. I was content to go on.

The weather held reasonably well for about half an hour and then released its load once again. I fumbled around and fetched out the ground sheet, this time to wrap it around myself and my rucksack to make an informal poncho. But plastic misbehaves in the wind and rain and I never quite felt comfortable with it. A few mobile buildings loomed up ahead, one of them open-sided with a panel raised. As I approached, it revealed itself as a milking parlour. Perhaps I could get a little shelter from the wind and rain there, and adjust the sheet before moving on.

I was struggling with it when a descending female traveller stepped off the track with an offer of help in French. She managed to pull the sheet down and around me, I thanked her and she carried on down the hill. I returned to the shelter, waiting for the rain to abate and I took the opportunity to roll a cigarette. Sometimes it helps to focus the mind.

The distant clanging of cowbells grew louder, one in particular, and I wondered if it was coming my way. I'm no country boy, but I thought cows were milked early in the morning and later in the day. When I heard a man's shouting voice, I made to move out of the way to avoid frightening any animals, or angering any cowherds.

The first cow to arrive gave me a dirty look. I told her there was plenty of room and she'd nothing to fear from me. Then a man opened the door of the nearest cabin, saw me, and ushered me over. I couldn't believe my luck: he was inviting me in to keep dry and warm. I stubbed out the last of the cigarette and shoved it into the bag I was using for scraps of rubbish.

I folded the groundsheet and left it on the floor just inside the door, with my rucksack. We made introductions and he invited me to stand by the stove. He was an Italian-speaking Moroccan, and came here on a week-on, week-off basis to help with the care of forty cows. I speak neither Arabic nor Italian, but he was fluent in French and I had a CSE in that. He filled a pot for coffee and offered me one, which I gratefully accepted.

I moved back to the doorway window to give him room and watched as TMBers streamed past going downhill in the rain, many looking very miserable. I stood in the warmth and I thought myself blessed. My host said something about how many Chinese trekkers were passing through here. I just nodded my head. He must have thought I didn't understand him and stretched his eyes with his fingers, with a big smile, urging me to respond.

Moltes, sí, I said, remembering that the Catalan for *many* was similar enough to Italian. Then, in Spanish, I added that they don't say *bonjour*, or *buongiorno* either. I think he understood, and he obviously liked me.

I have noticed that Chinese, Malaysians and Koreans, etc, most of whom travel in groups of 6–12, very rarely offer a greeting, and rarely responded to mine. Those that I encountered in the refuge seemed happy and smiley, but I never heard them speak any language I recognised. And why should they?

I only ever conversed with one East Asian on the TMB, and that was on last year's hike. She was travelling with a white American man, just the two of them, probably in their 40's. In the course of the past two or three days we had passed each other several times without speaking. At the Grand Col Ferret, as I was turning round to go back to Courmayeur, she was coming up. We laughed in recognition and she spoke English to me. We shamed the lack of visibility and I was telling her that there was nothing to see in Switzerland and that my trek was finished: I was going home. She didn't get a chance to respond before her companion, whom I'd watched struggling up the hill behind her, snapped *Come on!*, as he walked by, completely ignoring me. She scurried away apologetically with a hasty *Goodbye*. I felt like thumping him, but settled for a curse under my breath. I've never thumped anyone, intentionally.

English seems to be the unofficial second language of the TMB, in all three countries. It was the language I overheard other trekkers speaking amongst themselves as I approached them on the path. Despite that, I was never greeted in English.

Two more men entered the caravan: an Italian, the long-term tenant, and another Moroccan. There were more Moroccans in this caravan than I'd seen or would see on this entire Tour. Coffee was poured and the usual questions asked and answered. The rain was slowing and I wondered about leaving them to enjoy their break, but they were so friendly, offering me biscuits, and we had such a mixed up multi-lingual conversation, with everyone laughing, I didn't want to leave.

But I knew I must, so, after a while, making sure the rain had stopped, I stepped out again with a cheery heart.

Another few hundred metres up the hill stands another relic of borders and wars, converted to a small museum: la Casermetta. Drizzle started as I came alongside it, and plenty of others were sheltering there, so it made sense to take advantage and wait it out once again. There was even a luggage room to keep my pack dry.

Whilst there, I approached the warden, but he spoke neither French, nor English, nor Spanish. But he clearly didn't like the idea of me crossing directly from the Col de la Seigne to the Refuge Robert Blanc, at which point I began to get disheartened again.

I finally made the summit of the pass just after 12 noon – a climb of over four hours, which should have taken little more than one-and-a-quarter according to the guide book.

The exhilaration that I felt at this point, when crossing from France into Italy a year ago, was absent. It was disappointing to enter France with no scenery to enjoy, and disappointing that I hadn't covered any ground in the past twenty-four hours that I hadn't done the year before.

But I was still dry from head to ankle, with only my old boots taking on water. I congratulated myself once again for stealing that march the day before, asked someone for a photo, *sans* Chorkie, and girded myself for the long descent. The weather was no clearer this side of the border, but I still had options open.

Light showers came and went. Passing TMBers and I shared looks of irony as we wished one another *bonjour* on what was clearly not a good day.

An hour after leaving the Col, I turned into the collection of buildings that form the Refuge des Mottets. There was no one to be seen and I was ready for lunch. Then a middle-aged woman, who looked like she might work there, left one building to cross towards another. I asked in broken French if I might take shelter somewhere and brew up some tea. She offered me the outdoor picnic table under the canopy at the refuge entrance, and I thanked her from the bottom of my heart.

I spread out my things before realising what a potentially busy spot I was occupying. I was surrounded by rucksacks, sticks and boots, left by those currently indoors, presumably. People came and went, occasionally knocking the table as they put down or picked up their gear. A middle-aged hiker sat down opposite me to look through her things, and made it obvious that my gas stove was too close to her.

I had placed it just beyond the centre of the table, the best place I could find for my delicately balanced accident waiting to happen, whilst leaving me some room to prepare some food. I carefully picked off the saucepan and moved the stove back towards me, returning the pan to equilibrium without throwing near-boiling water over her, and she seemed satisfied. Five minutes was all it took and I had tea to go with a cheese and tomato sandwich. The rain persisted.

Presently, her husband joined her and we got involved in a conversation. They were Italian. He spoke a little English and I spoke a little Spanish, and it turned out that they too were heading for the Refuge Robert Blanc after coming from Elisabetta last night. I couldn't remember seeing them. After sorting out what she needed from her pack, the wife stood up and went indoors.

With the rain still falling and no signal to check the online forecast I was losing hope and 95% resigned to taking the 7km trek down the road to Les Chapieux (1554m amsl), where bivouac camping was permitted. It wasn't easy to accept, knowing that there would be no comforts, whilst a bed and toilet facilities were already paid for high in the mountain. But, if it kept on raining, I would rather an hour-and-a-half walk on roads with more options for shelter en route than four hours becoming more exposed with each step I took into the clouds.

I did my best to explain this to my new Italian friend, but he was upbeat, the two-day-old weather forecast on the refuge wall implied a dry afternoon. They intended to go for it and he insisted I should too.

His wife came back, anxious about the time, worried that they would not make it by 6 p.m., and they left me to tidy my things away.

As soon as I could manage with just tea and biscuit to hand, I stood my bag among the others and removed myself from the busy baggage area. Looking up at the sky, the clouds were more scattered and there were very few drops of rain. Lighting up a cigarette I challenged the heavens to drench me now and be done with it, or to clear up and stay dry for the rest of the day.

It stayed dry long enough for me to finish my refreshments. I learned that to use the loo meant removing my sodden boots to enter a dormitory building across the courtyard, and then having to put them back on again. A few spits of rain urged me back to the shelter of the canopy as I tried to put it off as long as possible. Ten minutes of indecision followed as I watched the skies begin to clear, and my enthusiasm for starting the climb grew – I could take the trail for an hour, and, if the weather turned bad again, there was still time to turn round – at least it would all be downhill to Les Chapieux.

Recharged in more ways than one, I clomped across to do what needed to be done. As I came back outside to put my squelching boots back on, I met the Italian man changing his boots for crocs.

I told him the skies were clearing and asked if they were ready to go, pointing up the mountain. No, he said, he had secured a bed here at the Refuge des Mottets. I felt disappointed for him, perhaps even a little guilty that I had talked him out of going up the mountain whilst he had talked me into it.

The time was 2.30 p.m., so I bid him *ciao*, rescued my pack, and left.

The fastest rate of climb I might normally achieve is around 250m an hour, way below the recommended rate for TMBers.

On that basis, I was cutting it fine to climb 900m by 6 p.m. It was equivalent to about 60% of the climb I would need to do on Saturday, so it could be prove to be a useful reference and measure of my ability.

The first half hour's walking is in fact quite easy-going, and the sun burned off most of the clouds. As I crested a small rise, the sound of trickling rivers in the distance was amplified to thunder and the most wonderful sight reached my eyes. Waterfalls and rivers too many to count fell across the mountainside directly ahead. They came together to form a single outlet in the valley to my right. I roused Chorkie from his torpor to witness this valley of a thousand waterfalls. [I later learned that this is known as Combe Noire].

Chorkie resumed his position in his preferred pouch and we set off.

As the path wound on, I began to have to cross some of the rivers, some with bridges, some without. As tiring as it was to climb, the elemental allure of walking upriver drove me on. All thoughts of turning back were forgotten.

The cascades grew taller and rivers washed along the paths, making negotiating them that much more delicate. I pride myself on having good balance, and I don't mind stone-hopping, but it is certainly more difficult to do with a heavy pack and when hungry for an afternoon snack. I missed my step and plunged my foot in completely on one occasion.

I began to suffer with breathlessness again. Checking my altimeter, I was under half way. A young couple caught up with me as I was bent over double, resting my shoulders. They were both dressed in brightly coloured lightweight clothing, like trail runners. He was tall and lean,

carrying a small pack, no poles, and looked athletic. She was much shorter, with a small pack and trekking poles. No sooner had we said hello and confirmed that we were all heading to the refuge than she offered me a pole.

I declined, with thanks. We chatted a little more about where we each came from – they were from the United States. We went to move on and I told them not to wait for me, I would slow them down. And, yes, perhaps I would take the offer of a pole.

Off they went, and I'm glad they did because, five minutes later, I slipped and fell headlong whilst crossing a relatively narrow stream on the flat, my first fall in eight days! So much for the stick, I thought. But no damage was done, except to my pride, and I forged on.

As I climbed through around 2400m amsl, I came upon some hikers with tents pitched on the grassy patches of a semi-level spur. For a moment, I wondered if that might be a good place to stop, but had second thoughts when I noticed all their belongings strewn out on the grass. In a French accent, one young man told me they had come across a steep pass that morning and a member of the group had injured himself quite badly. Added to that, their gear was all soaked through so they had laid it all out to dry. I winced, wished them well, and continued my weary way.

The Americans proved useful in marking out the trail for me, giving me something to head for as the path deteriorated still further.

Chorkie didn't relish another night in the rucksack, said he preferred to stay out tonight. I would need to come back down this path on the

morrow, so he found a cairn to his liking and we bid one another *bon soir*.

The last 200m of climbing seemed to be nothing but boulders interspersed with traverses across gently-sloping scree, with small patches of snow to break it up. It was hardly the tourist route the

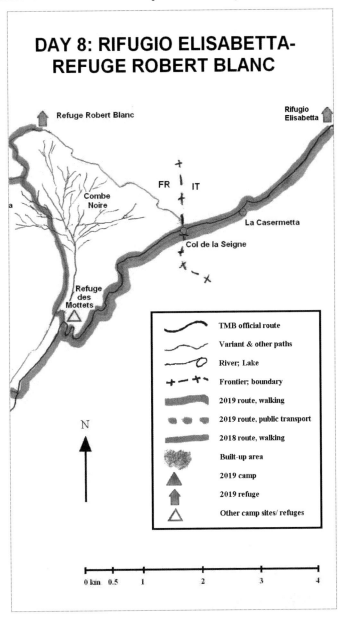

DAY 8: RIFUGIO ELISABETTA-REFUGE ROBERT BLANC

Refuge Robert Blanc

Rifugio Elisabetta

Combe Noire

FR   IT

La Casermetta

Col de la Seigne

Refuge des Mottets

	TMB official route
	Variant & other paths
	River; Lake
	Frontier; boundary
	2019 route, walking
	2019 route, public transport
	2018 route, walking
	Built-up area
	2019 camp
	2019 refuge
	Other camp sites/ refuges

N

0 km 0.5   1   2   3   4

warden had described to me. I wondered how bad the direct path had to be from the Col de la Seigne.

I finally made it to the refuge at 6.05 p.m. and was greeted by chickens. I couldn't have been more relieved.

Being so remote, water and electricity are precious at the refuge. Showers are not an option, with only one bathroom sink in which to wash. Tap water is taken directly from the stream and not recommended to drink, though what could taint it at this altitude I don't know. I drank from plenty of mountain streams if they looked clear. Bottled water is expensive to buy, as everything has to come in by helicopter. The refuge appears to be a highly insulated wooden building on a solid base, so I expect there is not much call for anything but a log stove in the dining/living area during the short season it is actually open (June–September).

I was shown to my dormitory, where damp clothes hung from every available hook, knob or handle. I returned to the boot room at the entrance, but that was the same. I only had my wet clothes from last night's washing line, and today's sodden socks that I wanted to air, so I found a space to lay them out there. My boots were soaking wet so I left them to air as best I could. Fortunately, I still had a dry pair of socks left for tonight and tomorrow.

I spent half an hour before dinner talking to a young Dutch couple. They had come over the same pass as the stricken group 400m below us on the grass. They said how steep the route had been coming up from Lacs Jovet and it was no wonder someone had got themselves injured. They conferred over its name – sounded like *dingen pass* to me – but they couldn't be sure. They were talking about the route I would have to take tomorrow if I were to go direct to the Lacs Jovet.

When dinner was served just after 7 p.m., everyone fitted around two tables. The warden reckoned he had twenty-seven bookings, but there were only eleven of us there that night, with me being the last to arrive. I sat with the young Dutch couple and another Dutch couple in their 30's. The Americans sat with four others who went to bed early for a 4 a.m. start.

It's possible that the other Dutch couple were on the track ahead of me, long before I met the Americans. I had seen a couple of people at a distance. They agreed to team up with their countrymen for tomorrow's traverse to the Col de la Seigne, that which I had been advised to avoid today. Taking a dangerous path is easier to face when you have companions in case of any potential accident.

We began with *Tomme de Savoie* cheese in soup, a surprisingly good combination. The soup was so good it was a shame to waste the remains of the pot, so some had seconds and I had thirds. A tasty risotto and a yummy dessert finished it off, but I was left wanting more.

The Americans joined our table after dinner. They were planning to start on the same route as me, but following the spine of the massif and stopping the night at the Refuge de la Croix du Bonhomme, close to the Col de la Croix. They would go via the Tête Nord des Fours, allegedly an excellent vantage point. I was tempted to do the same, but knew it would add considerable time onto my journey over tricky terrain.

I went to settle my bill ahead of the rest, and asked if the fire might be lit, on behalf of two of the ladies who were cold.

It was too late, I was told, as it takes a while to dampen down before bedtime.

I bought a 3€ can of cola, which left me little more than 5€ to survive on until I could reach a cash machine, the nearest being at Les Contamines, at the end of tomorrow's walk. Fortunately, I had some bread and cheese left in my pack, a packet soup, lots of cherry tomatoes, some milk for tea, and some biscuits.

I stayed up chatting with the three couples about various aspects of the TMB. We all agreed that the trail seemed to be busy, and someone reckoned there are moves afoot to limit numbers with the issue of permits. With so many people on the trail, the risk of environmental degradation was high. Unfortunately, I didn't get to learn how much progress was being made on the permits, or who was trying to get it organised, as the light was leaving the sky and it was time for bed.

My dormitory was similar to last night's, only it slept just twelve across two levels. With the four early-risers in another dormitory, there was plenty of room for the seven of us. As I lay in the darkness waiting for sleep to come, I thought of the Italians down at the Refuge des Mottets and the other fourteen hikers that didn't make it here tonight. I began to feel better about missing out on the Fenêtre d'Arpette. I wasn't the only one to wimp out of a tricky climb in bad weather.

Once again I slept well, this time without needing to get up in the night.

Day 9: Things Pass

The morning was bright and clear as breakfast was served. I did my best to empty the coffee pot single-handedly and to stoke up on bread and jam. I filled up a half litre bottle with tap water for the journey.

At 8 a.m. I was packing my still-damp clothes when the Americans entered the cloakroom to leave. I made sure to return the borrowed

stick, we wished each other well, and they set off just ahead of me. My boots were still sodden from yesterday, but with my thick dry socks on I didn't notice the damp till after I left the refuge.

I looked out for Chorkie where I'd left him and the path took us back down to where the wild campers had laid everything out the afternoon before. They were still camped there. I didn't pass close enough to chat, but tiptoed across the flooding plain above them, trying to keep the Americans in view. They were already half way up the impossible-looking slope.

It didn't turn out so bad, with a narrow scar threading back and forth through the scree. At the top, the Col de la Grande Ecaille (2751m amsl) was a bit unnerving, with what felt like a knife-edge saddle and 270° of horizon, but is probably closer to 240°. Being 1m higher than the Refuge Robert Blanc, this was now the very

highest point on my TMB that I would reach, even if it is not technically on the TMB. It is also 86m higher than the Fenêtre d'Arpette.

The harshness of the immediate slope ahead and down gave way to gentler terrain and a valley that I could see clearly across for over a kilometre. Another kilometre along it ran into the line of hilltops which form the spine of the massif, where the Americans were headed. I couldn't see them, though.

Looking once again at the map, I realised the Tête Nord des Fours (2756m amsl) would give unrivalled views down the valley North towards Les Contamines (1167m amsl), and up the valley East towards the FR–IT border and the Col de la Seigne.

They made the better choice of route, for them. If I had followed, it would add between 3–5 hours at my speed (as confirmed by a signpost a little further on), compelling me to bivouac at the Refuge de la Balme or at the Pont de la Rollaz, both marked on the IGN map.

Furthermore, it would take up to a further three hours to secure cash, buy food, and return in the dark to pay for the official camp site at Les Contamines. With no food in my pack for an evening meal, and no milk for breakfast, I had to head straight to town before the shops shut.

My path followed the Americans for a half kilometre more before taking a sharp right turn, upwards towards the Col d'Enclave (2672m amsl), the second point from which I could say it's all downhill from

here, the next highest point on my TMB being Le Brévent (2526m amsl) on the final day. But getting there involved another sharp climb of 250m or so.

Around halfway up it is the Lac d'Enclave, an ideal place to steel myself with a second breakfast-cum-early lunch and a cup of tea. Better to stoke my energy now before the last steep ascent for a while and certainly before the even steeper descent to follow. Whilst there, I used the last of the C.gas that I had left home with and the new one came into use. The empty tin would still have to be carried down to Les Contamines before I could dispose of it.

I lay back and stretched out in the sun, with my head cupped in my hands. For a moment, the lake reminded me of a hole in a Swiss cheese mountain – and I seemed to recall seeing Chorkie standing beside just such a hole with a pick-axe – but there was no evidence of industrial mining anywhere I'd been the past nine days, and Chorkie was still in his pouch. These mountains and valleys were probably picked clean of their riches by the likes of chamois hunter and crystal collector Jacques Balmat, and fenced through the likes of financier Horace Bénédict de Saussure, long before industrial mining became possible here.

Half an hour later I was at the top and marvelling at the view, with two potentially distinct landscapes to look at – the East-facing and West-facing slopes of the Mont Blanc massif – they were remarkably symmetrical, with a steep rock-strewn slope in the foreground, lakes in the midground, and mountain tops as far as the eye could see. Only the light seemed different on the ground. Above it, the cloud formations on one side appeared as negative reflections of blue sky on the other. It seemed like a good opportunity to try the 360° panoramic view option on my phone camera. It was hard to believe the view from the Tête Nord could be much more stunning.

If this was the tail of the massif spine, then I had gone around the neck at no more than 2040m amsl. Had I crossed the Fenêtre d'Arpette, that would have been a different matter. I could say that I had truly topped and tailed the massif.

Other people arrived and left, but no one carried large backpacks like mine. A middle-aged man with a small rucksack, and a young French woman carrying nothing, both warned me about the danger ahead.

Once I started, I wondered if I would have been better off with a stick, but, due to the steepness of the gradient, I could lean out or back to touch the ground with one hand – as a carpenter my hands aren't delicate – so I'm still not convinced of it. I certainly think that carrying two could have been more dangerous.

After fifteen minutes I realised I had strayed to the left of a spur of rock rather than to the right. I wasn't about to climb back up 20 or 30m, so I carried on, but found myself on a slippery scree slope. Gingerly, I tried to work my way around the spur towards where the path must surely be, but it was just as easy to go downward as it was to go across. In short bursts of descent, dislodging less by stepping lighter and quicker, from huge boulder to huge boulder, I kept some control. My erratic course was causing mini rock avalanches and I might have been embarrassed had there been anyone on the path below. Fortunately, there wasn't. I found a kind of equilibrium of my own, and, after about an hour from the top, the wayward path came into view from my right-hand side and the gradient relaxed.

The path led straight past the side of the largest of the lakes. On the far side as I saw it, a multitude of tourists sat as if at the beach, with parasols and picnics. I wanted a place to sit alone, to remove my trousers. I'd been wearing them non-stop for the past week, they were mud-splashed and I felt it time they had a good wash. I could dry my other wet clothes in the sun, whilst I bathed my feet and aired my now

dry socks and boots.

In most places, a black film seemed to cling to the rocks up to a metre in from the water's edge, but as I walked round I found a cleaner section, still isolated enough. My instinct for self-preservation must have been down with anticipation, for I suddenly slipped and fell on my right-hand side – just two metres from where I intended to rest. How could I have scaled that sheer drop and not hurt myself and then slipped on almost flat ground?

I quickly removed my boots, socks and trousers to look at the damage. I had grazed my leg just above the ankle and harshly bruised the muscle at the top of my thigh, grazing the skin in the process. Feet in the water, splashes to my leg wounds, a little anti-septic cream, no dressing, let it breathe, and I was fine. The trousers were unmarked, testament to their now-seeming invulnerability, and they went in the water for a wash with a spot of shower gel.

The first sign of a blister had come up on the back of one foot, probably because of wearing wet boots. Once I had finished paddling I put a dressing on it. I had a jam sandwich for second lunch, or whatever it now was, and got to work on the waistband of my trousers for the third time in the past week.

I nicked another centimetre or so and estimated I could keep this up another three times without compromising on comfort. F. would be proud. My brother, G., would have bought the 115€ shorts.

G. kept meticulous records of everything, so it was only natural that he became an accountant. As children, we began restaging an entire season of first class County Cricket matches, mainly with Subbuteo on the living room floor, but sometimes outside, with bat and ball, delegating rocks or camping chairs as fielders. He kept all the scores, ball by ball, but we didn't complete the season before he took up photography, and then record collecting. On hearing Deep Purple's *Made In Japan* for the first time, he bought a good stereo reel-to-reel tape recorder and cultivated record swaps among his friends. He built an extensive fully-catalogued library of rock music throughout the seventies. I benefited by default, as I got to hear all this great music, and attended concerts with him whilst my friends were still recording pop off the radio with a cassette player.

Our step-brother (almost two years my senior), moved into my bedroom after our parents married. He introduced me to George Orwell, but we grew closer whilst cycle touring on the open roads. I have him to thank for teaching me how to travel light. After University he became a corporate number-cruncher and a keen hiker.

I went through school alongside J., but we weren't close until our mid-teens. We followed different studies and attended different Universities, but the death of his brother just as I completed my studies

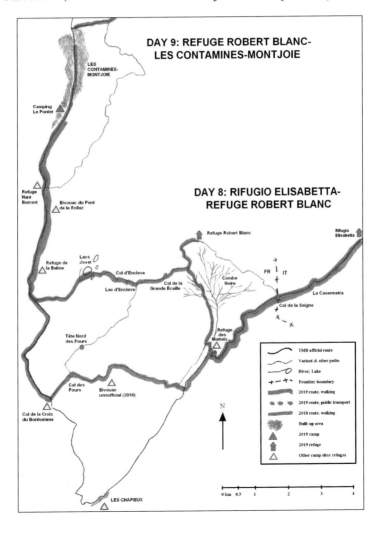

aligned us as drinking partners, best friends and soul brothers, which held good even when we were apart. Just knowing that somewhere in the world there is someone who thinks as you do is reassuring. But I roamed about and made other friends, like B., my fourth brother, not to mention the female sex.

Chorkie interrupted my thoughts to point out that my clothes were all dry, so perhaps we should move on.

Skirting past the multitude, we rejoined the trail as it followed besides cascades of water. I found myself walking much faster than everyone else, with great strides lengthened by my gravity-assisted heavy boots, emboldened by the dangerous descent of two hours earlier. Twenty minutes later, we rejoined the TMB just above the Refuge de la Balme.

Seeing an opportunity, I entered the refuge and asked for M.bars. They had S.bars, so I bought one and ate it. I immediately went back for another, leaving me only 50 cents to my name.

Walking on down the path, away from the refuge and away from school-age groups on the nearest knolls, I found a sheltered spot for my picnic of tea (from Lacs Jovet stream water) and chocolate. Ravenous hunger had become an issue in the past 24 hours, as an insufficient calorific intake was taking its toll. I am used to working long hours, but not every day without rest, and not without eating a lot more.

I glanced back for one last look at where I'd just come from. 3km away and 1km above me was the line of mountains that forms the spiny tail of the Mont Blanc massif, clearly marked against the skyline.

Twenty-four-and-a-bit hours ago I was at Refuge des Mottets. From there I entered Combe Noire from below, climbed to near its head and traversed out of it, across another combe and over the ridge of that before scampering down its outer wall and back onto the main trail.

I could have avoided all that traversing by sticking to the standard route: camping in Les Chapieux (1554m amsl) and walking up over the tail of the massif at a mere 2483m amsl, via the Col de la Croix du Bonhomme. The guide book estimates a 4–4½hr walk, or 6–7 hours at my pace (including breaks) to the Refuge de la Balme, which would put me in more or less the same place in which I was sitting at just about the same time: 3 p.m. If I'd followed the Americans to the Tête Nord des Fours, it could be any time from 6 p.m. onwards to this same point.

So, was it worth it? Of course it was, though perhaps next time it would be worth going direct from the Col de la Seigne to Robert Blanc and then to the Tête Nord, if I ever return.

Moving on, I forgot to take note of the Pont de la Rollaz site, but it is apparently on the right-hand side about 1km before the Refuge Nant Borrant, which appeared to me on the left-hand side of the path. The refuge looked like another one of those sketches by Hermann Hesse, an idyllic spot to enjoy a drink or meal in the garden. Since the Lacs Jovet, there were too many people on the trail to discreetly nip in the bushes, so I took the opportunity to ask a man serving tables if I might use their loo. He waved me inside and up a bare wooden staircase. Near its summit, Chorkie pointed out that I was entering the dormitory areas and I should have taken my boots off on the ground floor.

I persevered to the top and along the corridor, as quietly as possible, did my business, and made a guilty exit without being challenged. The building oozed rustic cosiness, reinforcing the good reports conveyed by my Kiwi friend at Rifugio Elisabetta. He and his partner had been here the night prior, and they enthused about the quality and quantity of food, as well as the comfort of the place. So it was one to note.

Somewhere around here is the turning onto a variant path that I had overlooked in my planning, and didn't see any signs for on the trail. It climbs into the hillside on my right as I looked down the valley and eventually connects with the Les Contamines–Les Houches variant. I

couldn't face any more climbing or distance than necessary, so I marched on down towards La Gorge on the standard route, invigorated by the gentle gradient, but irritated by even more slow-moving day-trippers, ramblers and amblers, like people who don't stand on the right on a moving escalator, but worse.

With the growing popularity of the UTMB and this apparent busyness, it was no wonder the subject of permits to walk the TMB were being considered.

When I was going anti-clockwise along with everyone else, I felt the same irritation descending from a hill at a pace as I passed the same people who'd left me for dead on the way up. Going against the flow, so far, this had not happened until now. It's not a pleasant sensation to recognise in oneself, and I know I miss more of the scenery by concentrating on what the person in front of me might do, and how to get past them. Perhaps I am selfish to want the path to myself? Funnily enough, the UTMB hadn't bothered me – at least the competitors knew where they were going, and I was the one holding them up.

For the week prior to sitting down for dinner at Rifugio Elisabetta, I had not been in company. I had spoken to lots of people, though quite superficially. In the past forty-eight hours, my encounters were deeper and the personal joy we each had for being in the mountains was contagious. I was sorry to have to say goodbye to some, but with a long history of relatively short friendships behind me I was used to it. There is something to be said for going anti-clockwise if, by seeing the same people at random intervals, one can forge close friendships, fleeting though they may be in the big scheme of things.

Perhaps my current negativity towards others was a result of my depleted energy reserves. Hermann had his moments of depression but, with the path to himself, he had no one to blame but himself.

La Gorge was quite busy with tourists without backpacks, as well as with those with, so I stopped only briefly for some photos of the rushing water and moved on. The Notre-Dame de la Gorge church stands back from the trail. I wondered if the raging torrents of water nearby provided any earth energy for the church to be placed on the edge of town and not at its centre.

This section of the TMB consists of mostly well-made level paths or tracks, commonly used by the locals and day-trippers. The stretched out town of Les Contamines struck me like one long happy valley of activity centres: all manner of fun to be done like water sports, archery, horse riding, skateboarding, fish and chips, etc. After my week in the mountains it was something of a culture-shock.

I marched on to the far end of town and found the Tourist Information Centre. I knew there was a free bus that left from there which followed the valley back to Notre-Dame de la Gorge, as I had used it to avoid the asphalt last year. I would get some shopping done and ride it back to the official camp site that I had seen somewhere amidst the pleasure zone. The next morning, I would get the bus back to the town to pick up my trail once again.

An ATM lay just beyond the TIC, so I availed myself of 60€ and went into the nearest supermarket, which happened to be a farmers' outlet. The C.cola here was 1.30€, to which I added locally-made sausages, cheese, strawberries and milk. I couldn't find bread to my taste, so nipped into the C.chain for some American sandwich bread and another bottle of C.cola, this time for 1.50€. Curses!

The abundance of plastic bottles that I kept buying meant that I always had one free to store milk in, rather than using the cardboard tetrapacks in which it is sold. It also meant that I could recycle the older ones as they became tired and less-hygienic with constant refills.

Le Pontet camp site was about 1km short of La Gorge, though entered from a parallel road on the other side of the river. It is big, not quite as big as that at Le Fouly, but big enough. The bus stopped right outside, and I went in search of reception.

The pitch cost 10.50€, my cheapest paid-for campsite so far. Hot showers were available, some garden tables and chairs to prepare dinner on, and wi-fi once again. My phone had not been connecting to the data network for two days, so that was something of a relief, if only to check on the weather forecast. It looked overcast for Saturday with the chance of rain, but tomorrow would be fine.

My battery charger was low again so I connected it to the mains in the toilet block whilst I went for a shower. The dressing I had put on earlier wasn't sticking too well but it would suffice. One of my smaller toes needed wrapping too.

I washed some clothes in the laundry basins provided and went to find the electric dryers. The price was 1€ for ten minutes, so I teamed up with another fellow who also didn't have much, and we shared twenty minutes for the price of ten each.

Excellent sausages. Very tasty.

Day 10: Speaking to Death

My first TMB began, like most people's does, in Les Houches. Rather than use the standard anti-clockwise path, I walked the variant via the Col de Tricot (2120m amsl) and rejoined the main path at Les Contamines (1167m amsl), then caught the bus through town and picked up the trail again at La Gorge.

Faced with walking from Les Contamines to Les Houches today, the standard route was my only alternative to re-covering old ground. However, Kev Reynolds isn't over-complimentary about it. The Kiwis at the refuge were divided. The girls loved it, and the senior couple agreed that it was scenic, but nothing compared to what they had encountered since. They recommended the variant.

The profile for the 16km hike shows a shallow but progressively steeper climb, cresting on the Col de Voza (1653m amsl), where the variant rejoins for the more sudden descent into Les Houches (1007m amsl). With a total of only 633m of climbing, it should be a stroll.

It felt like I might be going through the motions a bit, conserving energy for tomorrow's brutal climb, rather than just walking as far as I felt comfortable with. There was potentially time to climb half of Le Brévent by the end of the day, but with no camping permitted anywhere on the trail between Les Houches and Lac Blanc, today's fine forecast would be squandered. The limited legitimate options for camping and the completion of a contiguous Tour circuit as a goal in itself were at risk of eclipsing any enjoyment I might derive from *wandering* at my own pace. I would have to leave all the hard work to the last half-day rather than being able to enjoy it.

But there was nothing I could do about it. Chorkie advised me to relax and to make the most of today's fine weather while it lasted. I could enjoy a leisurely *wander* whilst keeping on course to complete the full Tour. Tomorrow would be another day.

My rucksack was slowly thinning out, so I could afford to do some last bits of shopping in Les Contamines to avoid the bother in Les Houches. I caught the 9 a.m. free bus back into town to buy some more farm-fresh sausages for this evening's supper. I could keep them protected in one of the empty cardboard cartons I brought for the purpose. Surrounding the carton with bottles of cold water and cola, they would keep well enough till needed.

French pastry is the best I've ever tasted, so I couldn't resist a cappuccino with *pain au chocolat* before I hit the road. It was a good opportunity to squirrel away some sugar sachets too, as my supplies were now at zero, and I didn't want a full bag. The irony that a kilo of sugar costs a fraction of the cost of a cappuccino was not lost on me.

On the bus back towards La Gorge, I disembarked where I had left the TMB path on my way into town yesterday. It led me down to the now-gently falling river, fed from the Lacs Jovet, among other tributaries. Once again I was relatively alone except for the odd local, sometimes walking a dog.

When hiking, I like to bathe my feet in mountain streams as often as once a day. Not necessarily at lunchtime, ideally later in the afternoon, when my feet are beginning to tire, and there's still a way to go. The ice-cold water helps to refresh and revive them.

But, like Chorkie said, we were in no rush today, so taking advantage of our solitude, I took third breakfast and bathed early. The plaster that I had put on yesterday had caught on my sock and was working loose. Best replace it.

I looked in the water, quite clear and noticeably colder in the shade of the trees, and my thoughts returned once more to the people that shaped my life before departing early.

My paternal grandfather died of cancer when I was 5, and my mother's father when I was 8. So I never thought it strange for my Dad to talk about death. One Monday evening, I was having my bi-weekly bath when he came in and said he'd read in the evening paper that a local man had died, and that his son went to my school. Did I know him?

Yes, I said, he was in my class. We never spoke, but he wasn't in that day, and I'd heard his father had died over the weekend.

My father then told me, as he had once before, after his dangerous driving incident, that I needn't worry if he were to die: the house would be paid for and my mother would be able to look after my brother and me.

The next day, he came home from work, had his dinner and went straight out to his weekly union meeting. He wouldn't be back before my bedtime. My mother followed him out shortly after to attend her yoga class, leaving my elder brother and me alone in the house.

Twenty minutes after she left, I answered a knock at the door. Two policemen stood there, asking for my mother. Before I could respond, my brother intervened, and I went back to washing the dishes.

My mother was not particularly late when I heard a car pull up in front of the house. I looked out of my bedroom window and saw her getting out of a police car with my father's mother, and I guessed what had happened. A tingling feeling washed over me, a feeling I later deduced to be a sign of intuition, not dissimilar to that described by my dowsing shop customer in later years.

The next morning I learned that my father been run down crossing the road to catch the bus, and that I didn't have to go to school that day.

Clinging to my mother at the funeral wake two days later, I listened to all the kind things being said about him. The one thing I took from it was that he was an honest man, who didn't mince his words, who spoke what he thought and was respected for doing so.

From that day on, nobody seemed to speak of him and I spoke to no one about him. When I saw my fellow fatherless classmate at school the week after, our eyes locked briefly in understanding, and we both got on with our lives without any further contact. I rationalised his death by telling myself that the law of averages meant that somebody's father, mother or close family member died every day. I was nothing special, so why not *my* father?

As I turned 20, joining the dots to his memory seemed important, particularly when trying to decide *who am I?* *What should I do with my life?* Honesty seemed like the best policy, at least with myself. Unaccustomed to talking about feelings with anyone, my isolation was the perfect breeding ground for nihilistic thinking and I barely scraped through my final exams with Honours.

I returned home to find myself consoling my school friend, J., after his brother died, but I was able to share my own grief for the first time.

The tenth anniversary of my father's death fell a few months later, during my gap year. I never intended to commemorate it, but Pink Floyd's *Dark Side of the Moon* was played at a party that night. I empathised with the despair and regret of the lyrics, with *ten years gone behind* me I felt that I had *missed the starting gun*, and faced the prospect that all that I touch will count for nothing once my lights go out.

When I later tried to convey to J. my frustration over my need to *do* something, it was clear that he wasn't motivated like I was. He was becoming a heavy drinker, whilst I could take it or leave it. He started going steady with a girl, and my itchy feet eventually got the better of me. I left for London, bought a second hand typewriter, and shortly met my own girl, who started out supportive of my attempts to write.

With no immediate fortune to be made in the writing business, however, I had to find alternative employment. Mincing my words, or just being agreeable, helped win me almost every job I ever landed. The Millennium came and went and all the optimism it generated soon turned to pessimism. With a few forays into journalism to my name, I was still no nearer to realising my potential as a writer. After five years as an independent self-employed retailer, I began to feel stuck in a rut.

On my fortieth birthday, my wife suggested we move to Spain. I thought: *Why not?* We should challenge ourselves, and our children.

On his fiftieth birthday, I rang J. out of the blue to wish him well. He was clearly down, and told me how he regretted doing nothing with his life. He'd had no children, and left no legacy, but he gave no inkling that he was seriously ill. He died of alcoholism-related causes six months later.

His wife asked me to speak at the funeral because he spoke more highly of me as a friend than anyone else. So touched, I tried to address his legacy. I spoke of his gentle nature and his willingness to say what he thought. He had good judgement and was supportive to those that deserved it, and despised those that didn't, and he let them know, either way. It was another reminder that I should begin to follow that example and have courage in my convictions.

A few years of learning Spanish, having to choose my words carefully, helped me lose some of my English reserve. I began to express myself more concisely than I ever had before, which, in turn, rubbed off in my use of English. But it takes a long time to break down the habits of a lifetime.

Shortly before he died, my step-father asked me if I was content being a carpenter. I said yes, broadly speaking, I was, though I didn't really mean it. He said he was pleased that I had found something I was

good at that I enjoy. It seemed to complete his circle of care for me and I didn't want to burst his bubble.

My father inadvertently provided for his family in the most extreme of ways, without much to show for it, so I just hope he would be pleased to see his son camping out, hiking, and being mostly self-sufficient, like a good boy scout.

I have two bright and intelligent grown-up children, each following their own respective passion, so they have my approval and I trust they feel that I have provided for them. But I still feel somehow unfulfilled: I may have worked on a few houses, launched a newspaper, opened a few bookshops, found thousands of books for customers in need, been a Parish Councillor, and done lots of other things for myself or for others, but I have created nothing I wish to be remembered for. I have *left no trace*, and for some reason that still that bothers me.

I looked across at Chorkie, still sitting on a rock by the river's edge, and wondered if inspiration would ever strike.

His lips were sealed and his belly full of fish, so I swept him up and said: *Let's go.*

Beyond Les Contamines the trail lifts away from the river towards the east and more hamlets with neatly stacked firewood. It was all very reminiscent of the walk between Issert and Le Fouly in Switzerland, though France seemed more affluent.

In between the hamlets there are sections of shady forest, and the terrain becomes more uneven. The awesome spectacle of the southern massif slid from view for the last time, as I passed through the unsigned hamlet of La Champel. I would have liked a last photo, one that many have probably taken before me as they approached from the opposite direction, but the sun was fierce and reaching shade seemed more important. I took lunch in one of the forested patches a little further on.

Crossing steep glacial rivers just before passing through Bionnassay added some drama to the journey, and helped to take the edge off the heat.

I was pleased to note that the eighteen porters that helped Balmat and Saussure with their scientific equipment are mentioned on a series of

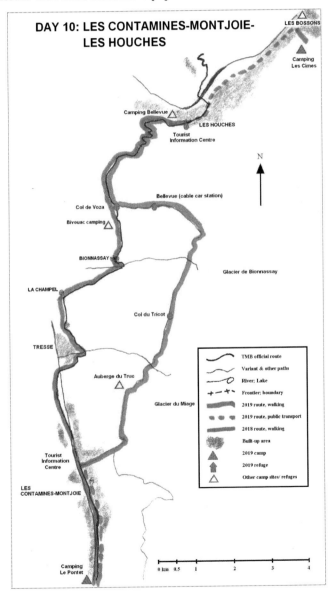

DAY 10: LES CONTAMINES-MONTJOIE-LES HOUCHES

information posts near Bionnassay. It never ceases to amaze me how the credit for mankind's achievements often falls to one person (usually a man), though they may only have been the one to complete a project, and/or oversee it, whilst the work of those that preceded or supported them is forgotten. Some may be gracious enough to admit their debt to others, but media (both historical and modern) worships personality, and typically celebrates the ego over truth.

From here on the gradient steadily increases in severity, but not so much that it caused me any problems. According to my map, bivouac camping is permitted somewhere around here, but the exact location is not shown. My guide book makes no mention of it, something which began to annoy me. Aside from the fact that the book was a three-year old edition when I bought it, I do wish it had more information for campers. The Cicerone guide to the TMB may be the most popular, but it is only one of many. To anyone thinking of buying a guide book for their own Tour, then I would recommend that they check the (revised) publication date and, if intending to camp, consider one better suited to campers, ideally with large-scale maps showing precise locations for authorised bivouac sites, and variant routes.

As the gradient steepened, I began to draw parallel with the spine of the Mont Blanc range and the peak of Mont Blanc itself. A whole different landscape came into view and it was all quite charming. Not at all disappointing.

I intended to stop for an afternoon rest and refreshment at the Col de Voza, where the variant path rejoins for the last descent into Les Houches. The Tramway de Mont Blanc stops here, though I'm not sure how regularly. I spotted a tram in the distance whilst walking the

variant last year, as it runs close by for a couple of kilometres, but I saw none on this occasion. The bar-restaurant was quite busy, and its presence alongside the track was a little unnerving.

I walked on a little to find a more tranquil grassy area in the shade of a tree to take some of my own refreshment.

Having now done both the variant and the standard path, I had to admit that the variant is more interesting. It passes up close to the Glacier de Bionnassay, there are more wide open spaces and fewer dwellings, but it comes at a cost – there are considerably more metres through which to elevate one's self – a difference of 832m anti-clockwise, or 585m clockwise. It was such a gruelling first day for me then that I couldn't make it all the way to Les Contamines and camped 4km short, near the Auberge du Truc.

I look back on that evening and remember how good it was to be wandering there, camping wild and seeing all this with fresh eyes. I shared the site with a German hiker half my age. We had met the previous night at Les Houches and he left me behind the following morning. He always walked ahead of me, but our paths kept crossing over the course of four days.

The Col de Voza was where last year's TMB really began for me. Seeing it again, it still seems fresh. Perhaps because the landscape is so vast, it really is impossible to take it all in, so there is always something

new to see.

Heading downhill on a winding path, the views become obscured by trees and buildings. The sprawl of Les Houches comes into sight, with only the brief glimpse of the mountains to relieve the disappointment I felt at entering another town.

Rejoining the main road, I turned eastwards towards the town centre. Some heavy building works were taking place and I marched past the temporary traffic lights, through the short tunnel they seemed to be working on, and looked for the left turn towards Bellevue camp site, where I had started from last year. It had cost me just 8€ for the night and was a real TMBers site, with basic facilities and very few big vehicles.

To my horror, it was *closed for improvements*. It looked as if a massive sports complex was being built there. Looking back up towards my left, it was hard to tell where the tunnel works ended and the camp site improvements began, with heavy equipment scattered across a large area.

I had counted on being able to camp here and now my plans were railroaded. There were no other camp sites in the vicinity shown on the map. What was I to do?

Despite being tired enough to welcome rest, I took solace from the fact that there was plenty of daylight left to find an alternative. My immediate thought was to plough on and find a secluded spot among the trees on the climb towards Le Brévent to prepare my supper and, when I could be sure there was no one around, pitch my tent just before darkness fell. It would give me a head start for tomorrow.

But first I had to go through the town proper to get to the foot of Le Brévent, so I returned to the main road and followed it. Half a kilometre along, I noticed signs for a Tourist Information Centre, and found it in a small shopping complex. In front of it is the official TMB Start banner, which I recognised from the many photos posted online by TMBers.

I made enquiries and learned there were six camp sites further up the road towards Chamonix. Six! There was no mention of any of them on my map, so I began to wonder how many other camp sites there are dotted around the peripheries of the TMB that I could have used. It was a 2€ bus ride away and the next bus was leaving soon from outside the door. I caught it and arrived at Les Montquarts (Les Bossons) stop as directed, just past a roundabout.

I stepped off, along with another couple who were looking for camp sites. They noticed some big brown signs at the roundabout directing us towards two of them. That's it, they said. Odd, thought I, as this seems to be the opposite direction to what I was told in the TIC, but there were no brown signs pointing in the direction I thought they should be. They seemed confident enough, so I followed them to the first of the sites only to find it *FULL*. I walked onto the other alone, further down the road, as they held back. It was also *FULL*. I turned back, informed them, and carried on past, frustrated by the restrictions enforced on campers, and swore to try and camp wild more often on any future camping trip.

Seeing a middle-aged couple pottering about in the garden of a café, I asked them for help. Back up to the roundabout by the bus stop and across the other side, up the hill, and there are three more, they told me. That's what I thought in the first place!

I marched off alone, crossed beyond the roundabout, beyond the parallel trunk road, and saw three more brown signs. These had the site's star ratings marked and I plumped for the lowest rating, thinking that might be more amenable to solo campers, and I chose well. Camping at Les Cimes cost 13,60€ and I could squeeze in between two fixed wooden chalets, pretty much like all the other small tents had between other chalets. I was given a free local bus ticket too, which I was grateful for, having nearly run out of cash again.

I took a shower, replaced one toe plaster, and added one to another toe on the other foot. Checking the weather forecast, rain was all the more certain overnight. I fed myself to the hilt and tried to stay positive, knowing that I had been lucky to get this far without major incident or accident, telling myself that the weather might not be that bad, but knowing I was being over-optimistic.

In the worse-case scenario, I would have to abandon my Tour and feel obliged to come back for another attempt – so near and, yet, so far. Fearing the worst, but hoping for the best, I fell asleep.

Day 11: Clouded Sky

Heavy rain woke me during the night, but I didn't need to use the toilet, so I slipped off to sleep again. When the morning light woke me, all was quiet outside. My back was aching again and I peered out to see nothing but cloud above the rooftops. My heart sank.

I put on some clothes and ran over to the toilet block before it could rain again, which it did, in bursts, on and off for an hour. In between showers I managed to get my breakfast and slowly but surely pack away my gear. My feet were beginning to look swollen, so I took another anti-inflammatory with a sip of water.

Sometimes I find it hard to swallow tablets, and this was one of those times. Thirty seconds later I coughed it back up and spat it out in the grass. They leave a nasty taste in the throat, so I wasn't inclined to take another. I'd rather go without. At least the plasters were holding.

After their final use, I disposed of my toothbrush, razor, soaps, towel, my worn-out gas fitting and other junk items in the appropriate recycling bins outside the site. I took my tent and ground sheet over to the spacious and well-equipped toilet block to wipe them down. I had hoped to be on the road by 7.30 a.m., but it was past 9 a.m. by the time I was ready. The full circuit was slipping out of my reach.

Fortunately, the back pain dissipated and I could put my boots on without too much discomfort, so I took no more pain killers.

A bus left for Les Houches at 9.30 a.m. and I wanted to be on it, despite having already resigned myself to not climbing the mountain today. At least I could return to Les Houches in order to walk back into Chamonix. Perhaps I could find the direct path up to Plan Praz to complete the circuit that way.

The mountain should have been visible, right in front of me as I trudged down to the bus stop. But the cloud persisted. I was almost in tears afraid that I might have to come back another time just for the sake of this one day's climb, if not to do it all again.

On the bus, Chorkie stared out from his pouch and urged me to rethink my calculations. With my thinned-out backpack, 300m/hour might be doable.

Based on 1546m of climbing and a half hour rest, a 10 a.m. start would get me to Le Brévent just after 3.30 p.m. With a 30–40 minute jog down 500m to Plan Praz we could be back in the town centre by 4.30 p.m. That made no allowances to stop to take photos, to take regular rests, or to take shelter, but we had another half hour to play with and there probably wouldn't be much to see anyway. I had a flask of tea prepared, so perhaps it was worth a shot. Furthermore, an escape route from the Refuge de Bellachat (2152m amsl), three-quarters of the way up the mountain, leads directly down to the cable car station in Chamonix, in case I needed to save an hour or more climbing.

By the time I disembarked in Les Houches, I was rejuvenated and ready to give it a go. The views would just be a distraction anyway!

I turned away from the Start banner and headed for Les Houches railway station without delay, passing it just before 10 a.m., determined to walk without stopping as much as possible.

The first hour or so was quite easy-going. Thanks to the denseness of the forest, the only distractions were near at hand like the giant statue of Christ the King, the odd rivulet to cross, or the occasional hand rails bolted to the rock. I passed a few hikers coming towards me, and one or

two came past me, but I didn't stop to chat.

Almost a couple of hours had passed when I emerged from the forest, where occasional pockets of clear air among the clouds offered tantalising vistas.

I took only five minutes for tea, biscuit and a smoke, and moved on.

The path grew steeper, and to keep me going I counted off the metres one by one, measuring ahead with my eyes slightly down. I double-checked my progress on the phone's altimeter and the height below the mountain top diminished in twenties and fifties. It was bordering on monotonous. Whether it was because I had a lighter load or because my breathing had improved, I didn't need to stop so often.

If only I could re-train my migraines to dissipate as easily as I had found it possible to re-train my breathing. No medicine ever proved reliable to prevent migraines, and the instant-relief painkillers aren't always instant – a nasty attack can sometimes wipe out a half day as I sleep it off.

MIGRAÑA
UNA PESADILLA CEREBRAL

ARTURO GOICOECHEA

DESCLÉE DE BROUWER

Several years ago, my GP recommended I try a radical new treatment promoted by a Spanish neurologist, Doctor Arturo Goicoechea. He advocates that, as far as the latest medical scanners can tell, there is absolutely nothing happening inside the body to be concerned about when a migraine occurs: no lesions, no inflammation, no clots, no cell necrosis, *nada*. He maintains that the brain erroneously sets off an alarm in the patient's head, and that the alarm can be silenced and the pain dissipated by the patient's own efforts. There are no triggers in the conventional sense, and it is not necessary to take painkillers and lie down in a darkened room, as per conventional wisdom.

He has published books (in Spanish) giving medical backing to his theory, and continues to promote it on his blog, well into his retirement. For his efforts, he is either ignored, mocked or ridiculed by almost every other doctor, medical institution, advisor, support group, or purveyor of pharmaceuticals. And, yet, traditional medicine has no better explanation and, according to patients, his methods have a high degree of success.

I liked the sound of this maverick doctor, and it seemed like he was saying that treating migraines was no more than mind over (brain) matter. I borrowed *Migraña, una pesadilla cerebral* from my local library and set about trying to understand it, by re-writing it in English. It helped, and I cut the incidences of migraine by half, stopped wearing sunglasses, and gave up the painkillers for over a year, by which time my incomplete neural re-programming was being re-subverted by years

of conditioning. And, last year, I was advised to start wearing sunglasses again as I am beginning to suffer from eye cataracts.

It was now nine days since my last incident, which I put down to tiredness, though I should know better that this is not the case. But knowing a thing and believing it, are two different things.

Around 12.30 p.m. the altimeter read 1820m amsl, so I was well over half-way up Le Brévent. I stopped for some lunch, taking just twenty minutes rest. I continued to make good time to the Refuge de Bellachat and treated myself to an espresso there, all I could afford with my once-again dwindling finances. Being alongside Mont Blanc, the view from this refuge is supposedly outstanding, but though I strained my eyes in hope, I saw nothing.

I was back on the trail by 2 p.m., marvelling at the ingenuity of the path builders. What could easily have been a dangerous ascent had been made easier by carefully laid loose stones. Despite that, I strayed from the path in thick cloud where the markings weren't clear and the path unmade, and realised my mistake when there was nowhere to go. It took me a few minutes to get back to where I knew the path had been, and forged on, finally cresting Le Brévent at 3.10 p.m.

It had taken me a little over five hours including rest breaks etc, and I couldn't believe my own strength.

There was no point in taking the five-minute detour to the restaurant and cable car station – the views were non-existent, I had no money for refreshments and I didn't want the cable car. After taking a quick photo of the signpost marking the high point of the trail proper, I carried on down towards Plan Praz.

Descending on a ski run, some eerie-looking cairns appeared out of the mist. Only two or three months ago, all this would have been

blanketed in snow, so I wondered whether they (and all the others I had passed the last ten days) were rebuilt every year or whether they miraculously survived the thaw. The outcrop on which they stood seemed to float in the mist, like a platter in the sky. I was reminded of Chorkie with the pick.

Twenty-five minutes from the top and around 400m down, the clouds parted and I finally caught the odd glimpse of what I had been missing. I tried to convince myself that I had seen it all ten days ago, so I should not be disappointed that the view was now so limited. But I knew that I would never get enough of scenery like this.

The cable car was just beyond, and I realised I had made it, a

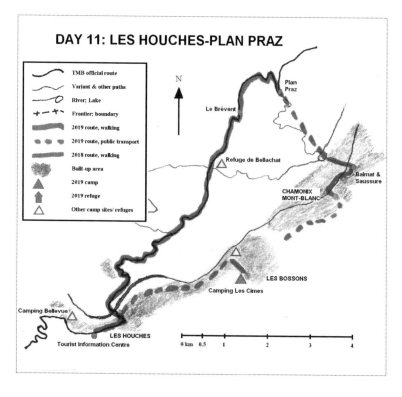

DAY 11: LES HOUCHES-PLAN PRAZ

TMB official route	
Variant & other paths	
River; Lake	
Frontier; boundary	
2019 route, walking	
2019 route, public transport	
2018 route, walking	
Built-up area	
2019 camp	
2019 refuge	
Other camp sites/ refuges	

contiguous circuit of Mont Blanc, and on schedule.

It was a disappointment to have missed out the Fenêtre d'Arpette, but I had otherwise completed the TMB, going above and beyond the standard route, without serious rush or panic. From that point of view, I had good reason to be pleased with myself.

I asked someone seated nearby to take a photo to record my arrival and to commemorate my personal achievement.

The main trail continued onwards towards La Flégère, but mine veered to the right if I was to catch my ride back to Chamonix.

I plodded heavily down to the Plan Praz cable car station, retrieved my return ticket from my wallet and was back at the Chamonix base by 4 p.m. From there it was a brisk ten-minute walk down the slope into town to say goodbye to Balmat and Saussure. Pre-occupied by the thought of food, I forgot all about Michel-Gabriel Paccard and went to find a supermarket, to spend my last 5€ on some carbohydrates.

**

Chamonix bus station was undergoing refurbishments and the building that houses the

ticket office and information centre was closed. Hoardings ran alongside, hiding something I never tried to see. A wooden kiosk not much bigger than a telephone box served as a temporary ticket office, and the pull-in area for buses and coaches was no more intrusive than a lay-by.

With plenty of time to spare, I made some notes on the day's adventure and some quick calculations: I had covered 175km in ten days and three hours and carried all my gear solo. I had climbed to over 2700m amsl twice, 2600m amsl once (albeit without descending very much between them), and over 2500m amsl on four separate occasions. My total climb was in excess of 10,000m, with an average gradient of 11%. [See *Appendix* for route details.]

I had camped eight out of ten nights. I had lost my balance and tripped only twice, and my wounds were superficial; my heart had raced and my breathing had laboured; I had eaten what I liked and smoked when I felt like it, but I didn't recall coughing once; my feet and back had been mostly pain-free; I had gone alone and yet been among friends at every turn; I had wandered with a purpose and faced down the contradiction. I felt in good shape for someone on the verge of being able to claim travel concessions.

At 5.30 p.m., a Swiss-run S.coach to Geneva pulled in, but that wasn't for me. My 17.30 connection didn't show, or, if it did, the driver didn't bother to gather all the passengers. At the ticket kiosk, the officer said she couldn't help because they didn't deal with E.lines. She could sell me a ticket to Geneva on the 18.30 S.coach, but no more.

Technically speaking, I had only a 50-minute window between arriving in Geneva and leaving again. The 18.30 would arrive too late.

I rang O.travel, and they transferred me to E.lines. They couldn't tell me why or where the bus was and, after much protest from me, suggested I sort myself out. I couldn't believe it. I would give the bus another fifteen minutes to arrive before ringing the agency back.

The coach never showed so I rang O.travel again. They said they could do nothing, offer no help and gave no assurances. It was down to E.lines. I was transferred again, but now the office was closed, it being after 6 p.m.

The kiosk was also closing, and I realised I had to take control. Having looked online, there seemed to be more than one coach per evening going my way from Geneva, so I bought a transfer on the 18.30 S.coach, and crossed my fingers. It cost just 15€ this time, even cheaper than the previous last-minute ticket, and I paid by credit card.

It was hard to think about anything else on the journey, so, having first switched to airplane mode, I prepared an email to E.lines to purge my frustration, and saved it to draft. Despite no noticeable delay at the Swiss border, we didn't arrive in Geneva until just before 8 p.m. I ran into the ticket office to explain my situation.

The ticket officer said I needn't worry. My connection that was due to leave Geneva at 7.20 p.m. still hadn't arrived from Zurich. They were expecting it any second now.

Unbelievably relieved, I went outside and waited with the dozen or so other passengers who had been there over an hour, but only for five more minutes.

Letting others board first, I went to pick up my pack, with passport and ticket in hand to show to the driver. Chorkie didn't want to leave Switzerland and he made a sudden bid for freedom, leaping out of his pouch to the floor. I was fortunate to notice, and, so that he didn't cause any more trouble, I picked him up, zipped him into my pocket, handed over the paperwork, and stashed my pack in the hold.

I found a double-seat to myself, untied my boots and removed them. We left at 8.10 p.m. and I tried to relax in order to soak up some of the sights.

I noticed the many different sizes and types of public transport sharing the same roads: single and multi-carriage trams on rails, some electrified, some not; electrified buses and bendy buses; all on top of private traffic.

I didn't expect to sleep until we were on the open road, so I was acutely conscious that after half an hour we were still driving around the city.

I decided to finish that email to E.lines, for it to be ready to go once I reconnected.

Just before 9 p.m., we rolled back into Geneva bus station. The co-driver announced that we had returned to pick up a delayed passenger on their way to Marbella, southern Spain. I wondered how many coach companies would bother to go back and fetch someone half an hour after they had departed, and I wonder if the panic I had felt in Chamonix earlier was misplaced. Full marks to A.bus, the coach service provider, for that.

When we finally left Switzerland, I thought once again of Hermann Hesse. He had been a bookseller, an antique dealer and a mechanic before writing his first novel at the age of 27. He became a writer full time and was eventually awarded the Nobel Prize for Literature at the age of 69. I have been a second-hand book dealer, a carpenter and a typesetter and have written nothing of note. I am being made redundant by the ravages of time on my body and the march of technical progress beyond my understanding. I have followed in Hesse's footsteps and *wandered*. I still have the hankering to be a writer, but my inability to see the trees for the forest makes it difficult to keep focussed on the details.

I fell asleep, reassured that there needn't be any further delays, and missed most of the en route stops, a strong indication of how tired I was.

Day 12: Fall Out

My head was spinning, like a cog in a machine; a hiker through the TMB turnstile; a whining blade through timber. Through the cycle of evaporation and rain, the cycle of the seasons, my spirits went from longing to satisfying and back to longing. Everything went in circles, nothing remained at rest.

The sun was up before we reached the Spanish border, but I didn't wake properly until we pulled into the service *area*. My feet felt swollen and I knew it was going to be uncomfortable to put my boots back on. I hobbled in to the restaurant to treat myself to a coffee and pastry, on credit card, and took them outside to enjoy the morning light and to smoke. With all that time on my hands while waiting for the bus at Chamonix, I should have changed into soft shoes and tied my boots to my pack. The anti-inflammatories were in my rucksack too, so I would just have to grimace and bear it.

I checked on Chorkie, he was happy to sleep, and pulled my phone from another pocket – Chorkie had plenty of likes, but there were no new messages.

Including this morning's breakfast, and assuming two small refunds on the extra coach tickets, my total expenses should amount to a little over 500€, not including equipment. [See *Appendix* for final sum.]

Leaving aside the coach costs, but including the pre-paid deposit for Refuge Robert Blanc, my total spend was around 365€. I had endured and enjoyed an amazing 11-day experience for 33€/day.

Back on the coach, I reflected on the people I'd met, and those I'd passed by or been close enough to get some measure of, surely over one thousand all told. I personally wished several hundred of them *bonjour* and entered a conversation with dozens of tourists and dozens of resident working people. From my observations, perhaps I could now determine whether or not I was a typical hiker.

Of the one thousand tourists, I estimated that 75–80% were white Caucasians. The other 20–25% were predominantly far Eastern in appearance (Chinese, Korean etc), with fewer than 1% Indian sub-continental, or of near Eastern origin, and even fewer black-skinned. Of the Caucasians, broadly a third sounded British, a third European, and the rest evenly split between Australasian or American.

Judging by this cross-section, walking the TMB does appear to be an indulgence for people from the wealthiest of nations, even if its participants are not necessarily the wealthiest among their own countrymen and women. I am unable to determine that, but as far as race or nationality was concerned I am very typical.

The male–female balance was no more askew than 60/40, largely due to male predominance among the sports: fell runners, climbers, bikers, etc. Likewise, the 25–40 age range probably formed the majority of people on the trail, thanks to these sporty types. Discounting them, I found a fairly even spread across the age groups, between the under-30's; 30–50's; and the over-50's.

As for rucksack size: there was a 40/40/20 spread between those carrying under-15 litres; 15–40 litres; and over-40 litres. Excluding children and fell runners, the older the hiker, the less they carried. Whilst there were plenty of individuals evidently older than I, they all carried under-40 litre packs, so most likely either day-trippers, weekenders, or refuge-users. My observations at camp sites illustrated that I was at the top end of the age range, as well as the top end of the pack capacity range.

If I were thirty years younger, then I would be quite stereotypical. But if campers represent as much as 10% of all TMB hikers, the over-50 campers can be no more than 5% of those (or one in two hundred). I encountered only two *maybes*.

I met only one smoking tourist, the *barcelonina* at Refugio Elisabetta, who might have been in her 50's, but she was not camping. I never noticed any TMBer smoking at any camp site. So I conclude that fewer than 1% of hikers smoke.

Without doubt, the vast majority of hikers follow the TMB anti-clockwise, so it doubtful that complete clockwise circuits constitute more than 10% of all full Tours, however they are defined. So, all other things being equal, if one among tens of thousands constitutes a stereotype, then I am guilty as charged. By my reckoning, however, as a camping, smoking, self-catering, over-50 person completing the TMB in either direction, I could be one of a handful, if not the only one in a season.

I can't be sure how much Chorkie's presence affects the statistics, but if the number of Instagram accounts held by travelling teddies, and the size of the cuddly shelf at Col de la Forclaz are anything to go by, I

suspect there are quite a few out there on the TMB somewhere – probably more stuffed marmots than real ones.

As a pairing, however, Chorkie and I may well be unique. So perhaps there is something to write about, because if I can do a complete Tour du Mont Blanc in my condition and at my age, then there's every reason to suppose that anyone can, or could, given the motivation.

This began for me as a way to escape from the mechanized world, to do some *wandering*, and concluded with me completing a *Grand Randonnée, because it was there* and because it seemed achievable. If I'd not challenged myself, perhaps I wouldn't have relished the *wandering* as much. But it felt like I had come full circle, as it has re-ignited the writing instinct in me. Perhaps there is room for some kind of *Homage to Zarathustra and the Art of Recycled Wisdom*?

Ever since I travelled in my youth, I became convinced that people are basically the same all over the world, and the apparent differences we place too much emphasis on, like race, skin colour and gender, are superficial.

At the earliest possible age we learn what is *mine* and what belongs to someone else – baby's rattle, daddy's hammer. Upon that foundation, relative prosperity and deprivation are inevitable. The conditioning and prejudices of our elders, laws, customs, and traditions only reinforce the likelihood of conflict. Babies are not born nasty and a good many make it to adulthood unable or unwilling to conform to the ethos that *more* (of mine) *is better*, and a good many adults are waking up to that after a lifetime of ignorance.

Like many tourist destinations, the Tour du Mont Blanc is in something of a bubble, isolated from the horrors of mankind's prejudices. But I had met people from all over the world and not once did I feel threatened by any of them. People can get along together once their agenda is reprioritised.

**

We arrived at my stop almost three hours later than scheduled.

I'd just missed the first bus of the day that would take me close to home and the next was not for few hours, so I phoned my wife for a lift.

She was still having her first cup of tea of the day. I offered to walk

across to the edge of town to give her a few more minutes to herself and a much shorter journey time.

Conkers came too, of course. Whilst I went in for a bath, Chorkie stayed behind to tell him how he'd seen Switzerland, climbed every cairn, fished every stream, exploited every photo-op, and featured in his porter's dream.

**

My right foot was swollen, but my left was fine. Some bruising remained on my hip, but otherwise I was in good form, with no injuries.

After a hearty meal out, I went home, sat back, and relaxed. In my sleepy state, something jarred with me and it occurred to me to check upon some dates.

Writing is commonly believed to have originated in Mesopotamia around 5,500 years ago, when accountancy was devised as a means to streamline a new tax system. The invention of the wheel was also around this time.

The benevolence of the wealthy towards the poor that existed until then transformed into a fight for riches, the rise of warrior kings, and chronic warfare, as the spoils were divided among the victors. The domestication of donkeys and the taming of human beings as subjects of the new kingdoms soon followed.

The wheel facilitated transport, and the opportunities for trade multiplied with the help of written debt. The wheel was fundamental to mechanization, whether being used in the pottery or in the movement of a clock; in the printing of the written word or in the mass production of anything we care to think of.

Writing's development into a graphical representation of the spoken language enabled scribes to expand its use: from recording financial transactions, to keeping an account of events, to writing holy scriptures, to registering laws, and so on. Nowadays, writing is most commonly used as propaganda by editors, businesses and governments, or simply to entertain the masses with complete fiction.

If the wheel was the building block of capitalism, then writing was the cement that bound it.

So it was not the invention of money per se, or even trade, which created extremes of wealth and poverty, but the creation of imaginary money in the form of recorded writing.

And I am guilty of falling victim of the need to write. But there are many other writers, some I've already mentioned, that used the media to record something of value.

I am reminded of *Erewhon*, a fictional, tongue-in-cheek attack on evolution theory by Samuel Butler, in which a traveller encounters a lost race of people beyond a high mountain range. Technology is limited to a point in its evolution (around the beginning of the scientific revolution, circa AD 1600) to prevent machines from gaining consciousness and taking over humanity. Written over one hundred and fifty years ago, the theme has since been done to death by science-fiction writers, but the process does appear to be happening.

The erosion of service in grocery buying is an example of how even consumers, not just labourers, now answer to machines. In my lifetime alone, shoppers have lost the shopkeeper's full attention and find themselves able to stock up, pay, and leave the shop without speaking to anyone, so long as they do as they are instructed by machines, whilst the staff work to refill shelves as instructed by computerised stock level monitors, and the boss is sat in an office 200 miles away.

The wheel of mechanization saves time and labour, and to keep up we must not waste a second of our lives: *time is money*.

But time is other things, unrelated to money, too. Escaping the wheel of money-creation is not a waste of time if it allows us to view the world from another perspective, from beyond the wheel. How our minds respond to that is down to individual character.

The weakest of us may go off at a tangent into the realms of madness, but if one can escape the hamster wheel and be indifferent to its effects, if only for a short while, we can see things for what they really are. We have a chance to recognise that all the human tendencies which we may consider virtuous risk being sacrificed on the wheel, in an endless quest for more of everything, with the least effort, in the shortest time possible.

**

I am almost forty years older than the boy I was when I told my mother I wanted to write. Having to some extent sacrificed my principles and kept my own counsel to gain experience, as well as to make ends meet, I have only confirmed that what I suspected back then to be important remains important today – not just to me, but to others.

More than a lack of experience, I lacked the vocabulary to express what I felt I knew, and the courage in my convictions to say it. But it is only by disengaging one's cogs and shifting gear, by seeing the world through another's eyes, on a regular basis, that we get to know our selves and earn the right to say *This is me, I see things differently, so let's talk about it.*

Appendix: Checkmate

Weight measurements are in grams.
    ** Italicized items are either worn or carried independently of the rucksack, so do not feature in the final pack weight.

PACKING LIST 1/3

Item	2018 Weight	2019 Weight	2018 Cost	2019 Cost	Origin & Comments
Vitals packed:					
Rucksack & cover	1800	1800	70 €		Amazon, August 2018
Tent	1700	1950	80 €		Blacks, Oct. 2019
Ground sheet		177			Salvaged
Sheet sleeping bag	265	265			c.1970's, in plastic bag
Sleeping bag	2430	840		29 €	Amazon, March 2019
Emergency blanket		61		3 €	Decathlon, June 2019
Roll mat in bag	267	267			c.1980's
Vitals to hand:					
Chorkie		43			Passenger
Bungee		93			c.1990's
Foam skating		138			Salvaged
Map	67	67	8 €		Amazon, Aug. 2018
Guide book w/o sleeve	287	271	20 €		Chamonix, Aug. 2018
Compass	25	25			Found
Head torch	72	72			Amazon, 2017
Roll multi-purpose tape		70			c.2010
Chargers & Cable	303	303	12 €		Charger, Aug. 2018
Whistle		12		1 €	1€ shop, June 2019
*Camera ** *	230				
*Walking sticks ** *	580	290	34 €		Les Houches, Aug. 2018
*Passport ** *	35	35			
*Phone ** *	170	189		145 €	Esdorado, July 2019
*Cigarettes & lighter ** *	100	100			
*Purse ** *	80	80			Salvaged
*Wallet ** *	72	72			Gift
Cooking					
Thermal rucksack		466			c.2005
Beer towel / Tea Towel	210	118			Salvaged
Flask empty	275	277	8 €		Andorra, Dec. 2018
Café mug	200	186	12 €		Zyliss, May 2019
Kettle & gas fitting	311	311			c.1990's
Cutlery	150	93	3 €		Ceramic knife, Jul. 2019
Pringles tube container x3		141			Salvaged
Empty drinks bottles x3	75	75			Reused
C.gas	625	355	5 €		Decathlon, June 2019
Plates, dish, pans	800	660	14 €		Online, new, August 2018

PACKING LIST 2/3

Item	2018 Weight	2019 Weight	2018 Cost	2019 Cost	Origin & Comments
Clothing					
Boots **	2300	2300			c.1981
Clothes to be worn **	1220	909			c.2017 or earlier
Extra long sleeve shirt	334				c.2010's
Hat	180	31		4 €	Decathlon, June 2019
Coat	579	579	80 €		North Face, August 2018
Gloves	85	43			c.1990's
Sun glasses in case	125	75		49 €	Apr. 2019, Prescription pair
T-shirts	500	129			c.2017
Gilet	600	567		34 €	Blacks, new, Winter 2018/19
Extra Handkerchiefs	31	31			c.2010's
Soft shoes	550	559			c.2016, in plastic bag
Trousers (& shorts)	500	238		10 €	Decathlon, June 2019
Extra Socks	220	181		36 €	Decathlon/Blacks, Winter 2018/19
Extra Underpants	280	144			c.2018
Health & hygiene					
Bath towel in bag	390	371			Salvaged
Toothbrush & paste	70	63			
First aid & pharmaceuticals	110	118			
Needle/Thread	1	1			
Toilet roll	150	46			Part roll for emergency
Insect repellents	250	84			
Shaving equipment	200	55			
Shower gel / Shampoo	50	43			Hotel freebies
Clothes pegs (x4)		18			
Food/drink (see next page)	5018	5947			
Total	24872	22434			
*** Less items worn/carried*	4787	3975			
Pack weight leaving home, inc. food/water	20085	18459			
			318 €	339 €	**TOTAL NEW SPEND FOR ITEMS USED**
			92 €	248 €	*Less personal items*
			100 €		*Less birthday donations*
			126 €	91 €	**NET SPEND ON REUSABLE EQUIPMENT**

PACKING LIST 3/3

Item	2018 Weight	2019 Weight	2018 Cost	2019 Cost	Origin & Comments
Food essentials					
Cigarettes/tobacco	90	90			in manufacturer's packaging
Tea/coffee	150	130			inc. 50g plastic jar
Sugar	250	242			inc. 50g plastic jar
Margarine	150	85			inc. 5g plastic pot
Muesli	350	515			inc. 15g bag
Biscuits – home-made	200	269			inc. 12g plastic container
Salt/pepper/coffee	8	9			in Pringles tube listed above
Onions/peppers	200	108			in Pringles tube listed above
Soups	70	155			in manufacturer's packaging
Assorted snacks	200	127			in manufacturer's packaging
Bread	150	390			inc. 5g bag
Milk (2x 215g + 500g)	500	930			inc. 2x 15g cartons
Meat	200	204			in Pringles tube listed above
Cheese	100	75			in Pringles tube listed above
Cake – home-made	200	240			in Pringles tube listed above
Tomatoes	150	210			in Pringles tube listed above
Jam		108			inc. 5g plastic pot
Tuna		210			in manufacturer's packaging
Pasta	100				
Water (500g x2)	1500	1000			in bottles listed above
Cola in 1l bottle		400			
Food/drink for the road	450	450			in flask listed above
TOTAL FOOD & WATER	**5018**	**5947**			

ROUTE BY DAY

		Km	hrs	m
0	21.10h Bus–Chamonix 11.30h			
1	Chamonix–Cable car–Plan Praz–La Flégère–pond	8	5.5	300
2	Pond–Lac Blanc–Aig. Posettes–Ref. Les Grands	19	11	1300
3	Ref Les Grands–Alp Bovine–Champex-Lac	20	6.5	780
4	Champex-Lac–Le Fouly	16	4.5	550
5	Le Fouly–Grand Col Ferret–Arp Nuova–Bus–Hobo	16	6	1150
6	Bus–Arp Nuova–Tête Tronche–ND Guérison–Bus–Hobo	23	8	1100
7	Bus–ND Guérison–L. Chécrouit–Ref. Elisabetta*	17	4.5	1100
8	Ref. Elisabetta–Ref. Mottets–Ref. Robert Blanc	13	6	1220
9	Ref. Robert Blanc–L'Enclave–Lacs Jovet–Les Contamines	14	7	350
10	Les Contamines–Les Houches–Bus–Les Bossons	16	4.5	633
11	Bus–Les Houches–Plan Praz–Cable–Chamonix	13	5	1546
12	Home 8.30h			

	Km	hrs	m
Net Distance; Time; Altitude	175	68.5	10029
* Extra distance walked Day 7	7	2	450
Totals	182	70.5	10479

COSTS

Following my email, E.lines requested that O.travel refund my credit card for the transport failings. I received a full Sterling refund to my Euro-based credit card, bringing the net cost of transfers to 45€.

Food & drink costs do not include those items I started with – it probably amounts to around 10€.

	2018	2019
Food & drink	129,34 €	139,91 €
Local transport	32,85 €	32,00 €
Camping costs inc. Laundry	58,90 €	82,80 €
Refuge costs	0,00 €	110,45 €
TOTAL COST ON TOUR	**221,09 €**	**365,16 €**
TRANSFER COSTS	151,00 €	45,00 €
REUSABLE EQUIPMENT (see above)	126,00 €	91,00 €
OVERALL COST	**498,09 €**	**501,16 €**

Acknowledgments: Do Not Forsake Me Oh My Darling

I am particularly indebted to both Hermann Hesse, for *Wandering* (1920), and to Patrick McGoohan's *The Prisoner* TV series (1967), for their inspiration, and for my chapter titles.

My personal thanks are due to J.F., who unwittingly inspired me to write something of myself after we met in a parking bay last year; to my Catalan friend, S.C., who proof-read an edit and whose comments encouraged me to persevere; to my wife, C., who offered advice on content; and to my son, K., who was rooting for Chorkie from the start and continued to provide encouragement throughout the writing process.

I was hoping to have completed this book by Christmas 2019. However, late in November, my mother fell ill, was hospitalised, and died three weeks later.

This upset my schedule, and, upon returning to the work of editing, I realised that I had neglected to include her influence upon me. This may be because she was always constant, an anchor of kindness and love that I, for one, took for granted.

It behoves me to suggest that, whilst my fathers, brothers, and friends influenced my impulses and my will to wander in one way or another, my mother instilled in me all the virtues that form the bedrock of all that I am.

I also have her to thank for introducing me to Chorkie, without whom this tale would surely have been less interesting.

Rest in peace Mum.

K.R. Allcoat, March 2020

Printed in Great Britain
by Amazon

72512971R00078